BUSINESS DEVELOPMENT
THAT WORKS

BUSINESS DEVELOPMENT THAT WORKS

PRACTICAL STEPS TO ENHANCE
YOUR PERFORMANCE IN SALES
AND BUSINESS DEVELOPMENT

RICHARD WOODWARD

First published in 2013 by Richard Woodward and Associates PTY LTD
PO Box 908 Bondi Junction Sydney NSW Australia 2022
www.richardwoodward.com.au

Publishing services provided by GOPublishing, an imprint of Green Olive Press
www.greenolivepress.com

National Library of Australia Cataloguing-in-Publication entry

Author: Woodward, Richard.
Title: Business development that works: practical steps to enhance your performance in
sales and business development / Richard Woodward.

ISBN: 9780987377401 (pbk.)

Subjects: Sales management. Organisational effectiveness. Success in business.

Dewey Number: 658.1

Cover and internal design: Gloria Tsang/Green Olive Press
Printed in Australia by Vanguard Press

Acknowledgements

Thank you to all the inspirational people and great organisations I have been fortunate to work with. Particular thanks to Caroline Webber and Robert Gerrish for their advice, guidance, encouragement and support throughout the development of the book.

CONTENTS

INTRODUCTION

There is a reason people succeed in sales and business development

For over twenty-five years, I have had contact with thousands of people engaged in sales and business development.

What I have observed, and continue to observe, is that too many people struggle unnecessarily to get the results they need. In turn, their struggle has a serious impact on their careers, their organisations and their families.

For people in commercial roles, success or failure in sales and business development can mean the difference between gaining promotion or being shown the door because they failed to reach their targets. For people representing charities, success or failure in sales and business development can mean the difference between securing funds to provide services to those in need or not. For people running their own business, success or failure in sales and business development will determine whether they can provide for their family and achieve their business goals and dreams.

My experience has given me insight into why some people are successful in sales and business development roles and why others are not.

Unsuccessful business developers typically lack an effective process and they lack the required attitude, skills and knowledge necessary for securing clients. Worse still, unsuccessful business developers repeat activities that don't generate a positive outcome meeting after meeting, phone call after phone call, pitch after pitch, time after time.

This does not have to be the case.

With more thought and planning, together with proven practical advice on what's best to do at each stage of the sales and business development process, the results and the experience of unsuccessful business developers can be dramatically turned around.

Effective sales and business development is about doing the right things, every time

Effective business developers use a clear process and display the right skills, knowledge and attitude time after time. The right skills include questioning, listening, writing and presenting, with the right knowledge of their proposition, audience, competitors and market. Effective business developers are enthusiastic, professional, persistent and confident.

If you want to enhance your performance in a business development or sales role, this book is for you

Whether you are starting out in a sales and business development role for the first time or if you are an experienced campaigner looking for a refresher, this book will guide you step-by-step through the key stages of the sales and business development process. It contains proven tips on what to do at each stage to ensure you get the results you need to identify, secure and retain the people you want to do business with – your ideal clients. At the end of each chapter, the key points are summarised and there are exercises for you to undertake which will allow you to apply my advice to your own specific situation. A notes page is provided where you can capture your thoughts.

This book is a culmination of my years of experience working in key business development roles, running my own business, training others and observing what does and doesn't work. By following the proven tips and techniques I have developed along the way, you will enhance your sales and business development performance and will be better positioned to achieve the outcomes you want.

I wish you all the best on your journey to achieving success… and business development that works.

Richard Woodward

ABOUT THE AUTHOR

Richard Woodward is a business development strategist, trainer and speaker who works with dynamic organisations to help them gain new business.

His clients range from major corporates and small to medium businesses to leading organisations in the worlds of arts, sports, charities and events.

Richard facilitates strategy sessions and planning days to ensure clients have robust plans that work and inspire the organisation; provides business development, sales and presentation training to ensure people can implement their plans; and delivers keynote presentations at conferences and events.

Prior to establishing Richard Woodward & Associates in 2004, Richard worked in sales, marketing and business development roles for the Commonwealth Bank, Sydney Opera House, KPMG, the Royal Automobile Club, Stadium Australia and McCarthy & Stone.

Richard lives in Sydney, Australia.

GLOSSARY

Business development – a strategic approach to developing new business and growth opportunities, typically comprising a range of tasks and business processes including sales, marketing and customer service.

Business development activity plan – a plan outlining the activities, responsibilities and timings that will enable you to identify and attract a sufficient quantity of prospects to convert into clients and achieve your targets.

Client – a person or business who uses your products and services or who provides a contribution to your organisation. Different organisations have unique terms for who they do business with. A client may be known variously as a customer, sponsor, donor, exhibitor or member. My use of the word *client* covers all of these terms.

Conversion rates – the rate at which you convert your prospects into meetings and then into clients, i.e., 10:5:1. (See also *Pipeline*.)

Elevator pitch – a concise summary of your service, business or program used to create interest and attract your ideal clients. It is called an elevator pitch from the idea that if you get in an elevator with someone and they ask you what you do, you only have a brief amount of time to attract their interest before one of you steps out.

Lifetime value – the total dollar value realised from a client over the course of a relationship.

Long term – sales beyond the financial year in which you are looking to secure or retain a client.

Non-verbal communication – unspoken communication delivered through posture, gesture, eye contact, facial expression and appearance.

Pipeline or sales pipeline – placing prospects at different stages of the sales process and measuring their progress through the pipeline from unqualified prospect to client.

Prospect – a potential client.

Proposition – a statement of the outcomes or experience that you will deliver for your client.

Qualified prospect – an ideal potential client; someone for whom you believe you can provide a solution to their needs.

Return On Investment (ROI) – tangible outcomes measured against the investment. ROIs may measure more than just financial return.

Revenue – gross dollar return from a client.

Search Engine Optimisation (SEO) – methods used to boost the ranking or frequency of a website in results returned by online search engines in an effort to maximise user traffic to the site.

Short term – the current or next financial year in which you are looking to secure or retain a client.

Social media – websites and other online communication tools used by large groups of people to share information and to develop social and professional networks.

State management – the ability to influence and manage your mindset or state of mind at any moment to achieve the task at hand.

SWOT analysis – a structured planning method used to evaluate the strengths, weaknesses, opportunities and threats involved in a business or project.

Targets – the number of clients and the amount of revenue you are looking to achieve in any given time period.

Traditional marketing – activities such as print and television advertising, direct marketing and exhibiting.

Unique Selling Point (USP) – one aspect of your business, product or service that sets you apart from your competition and provides your prospects with a good reason to choose you over your competitors.

Unqualified prospect – a potential client you have identified in the course of your business development activity who you have yet to evaluate.

Visualise – using your imagination to picture specific aspects of the business development process such as your desired performance and the outcomes of your next presentation or meeting, i.e. to see, hear and feel yourself speaking in a confident, engaging and assertive manner, with your prospect responding positively to your proposal.

EFFECTIVE BUSINESS DEVELOPERS

Why is it that some people are effective at business development and others are not? The explanation is found in their actions – what they do or do not do. Effective business developers have an effective process; a sequence of activity that they move through successfully completing one stage of the process before moving on to the next.

Effective business developers:

- Identify their ideal client
- Develop their proposition
- Find prospects
- Refine prospects
- Approach prospects
- Attract prospects
- Prepare for a sales meeting
- Build rapport
- Uncover needs
- Explore solutions
- Present compelling solutions
- Close the sale
- Service and retain clients
- Maximise their performance at every stage

In this book, I will guide you, step-by-step, through each stage of this process.

Effective at every stage

Effective business developers are effective at every stage of the process. It's no use:

- Being a great presenter if you haven't uncovered your prospect's real needs

- Being the great discoverer of needs if your approaches don't get you in front of enough qualified prospects

- Having great approaches if you haven't identified the right people to approach

- Approaching anyone if you don't have a proposition which will meet their needs – you will be wasting their time as well as yours

People who do not make successful business developers often make these mistakes.

Required Attitudes, Skills and Knowledge (ASKs)

As well as needing an effective process, effective business developers need the right attitudes, skills and knowledge, and need to use these throughout the process.

Attitudes you need to display

Effective business developers display the following attitudes:

- **Confidence** – displaying confidence and giving the prospect the confidence to buy from them

- **Passion** – for their business, organisation, product and service

- **Belief** – in what they have to offer and that they can provide a solution to their prospect

- **Initiative** – in identifying relevant contacts and information

- **Creativity** – when developing approaches and presenting solutions

- **Flexibility** – when exploring solutions to their prospect's needs

- **Professionalism** – in the way that they conduct themselves at all times

- **Determination** – to succeed

- **Persistence** – taking the knock backs, being resilient and carrying on until they get a sale

- **Positivity** – throughout the business development process

- **Consistency** – apply the right attitudes, skills and knowledge in all situations at all times

- **Attention to detail** – in everything they do

Of course, this list is not exhaustive.

Required skills

Effective business developers have the following skills:

- **Research** – sourcing and analysing relevant information to gain knowledge

- **Communication** – both verbal and non-verbal used when engaging prospects

- **Rapport building** – whilst building rapport is more a stage of the process than a skill – verbal and non-verbal communication skills are the actual skills used in building rapport – I have listed it as a skill as it's such an important activity within the process

- **Questioning** – the number one skill for all business developers as it is used throughout the process in approaches, building rapport, uncovering needs, presentations, closing and servicing

- **Active listening** – used at the same time as questioning skills

- **Writing** – writing quality prospect approach letters, proposals and marketing materials

- **Presentation** – presenting your ideas and proposal to the prospect

- **Negotiation** – negotiating the terms of the arrangement

- **Organisation** – organising your resources to be effective in business development

- **Project management** – managing multiple prospects and clients at the same time

- **State management** – accessing a positive mindset on demand

- **Financial management** – calculating and analysing the financials, and managing the finances to achieve the financial objectives

Knowledge – what you need to know

Effective business developers have a clear understanding of:

- **Their target audience** – the objectives, needs and hot buttons of the companies and people they approach

- **Their own organisation** – its mission, vision, history and values

- **Their product or service offering** – the features and benefits and proposition for each of the product and service offerings

- **Their competitors** – their strengths and weaknesses in relation to their competitors, and their Unique Selling Point (USP)

- **The market** – industry trends and pricing for comparable offerings in the markets in which they are competing

- **The economic environment** – whether the economy is contracting or expanding (this may influence their pricing strategy)

- **The numbers** – targets, costs and margins, and budget vs. actual year to date

- **Their plan** – to achieve their targets

Attitudes, Skills, Knowledge: All three are required

Effective business developers display the required attitudes and skills and knowledge in equal measure. An absence of any of the above is a major barrier to success. It is no use being passionate (attitude) but not understanding the market (knowledge) or being unable to present your proposition (skill). Likewise, if you are passionate and have a strong proposition but are unable to effectively present the opportunity you will still not be successful.

So let's get into the first stage of the process, identifying who you want to do business with – your ideal client.

1 | IDENTIFYING YOUR IDEAL CLIENT

The key to successful business development is to have absolute clarity about who you want to do business with and who you are looking to attract. Depending what industry you are in, you will have your own term for who this is. It may be a client, customer, sponsor, donor or exhibitor. Throughout the book I have used the phrase 'ideal client' to cover all scenarios.

Initial consideration of your ideal client will have evolved from a SWOT analysis – an evaluation of your internal strengths and weaknesses, such as your skill set and experience, and of external opportunities and threats to your business, such as market potential and competition.

Identifying your ideal client is important for three reasons:

1. **It enables you to focus your resources**
   Most of us have limited resources in terms of time, budget and energy. The greater your clarity, the more focused and effective you can be in allocating your resources to engage your ideal clients and avoid wasting time, budget and energy attempting to engage those who are not ideal.

2. **What you focus on, you will attract**
   If you focus on engaging your ideal clients, you will attract the kinds of people and businesses that you want to work with; those that will enable you to develop a sustainable and profitable business or organisation, and one that is enjoyable to work in.

3. **You will get referred**

   If you do a great job for your ideal client you stand a greater chance of being referred to similar people and organisations in his or her network. This means you will get to work with more of the same type of people and organisations – your ideal clients. On the other hand if you don't have this clarity and you use your limited resources to undertake activities that engage audiences that are not your ideal, such as agreeing to speak at an event where your ideal clients are not present, you risk attracting people that are not your ideal clients. If you then do a great job for them they will refer you to similar types of people.

Identifying your ideal client

The key is to have a clear mental picture of your ideal client. Two questions that can help you to develop this image are:

1. Which of your existing clients would you prefer to do more business with, and why?

2. Which of your existing clients would you prefer to do less business with, and why?

The more detailed you can be with your answers, the greater clarity you will have about who you want to work with. Consider the questions from both business and individual perspectives. What types of businesses do your preferred clients work in? Consider the industry sector, geographical location and budget at their disposal. What type of people are they? For me this point is very important. I like to work with people that are committed to improvement, see training as an investment and are enjoyable to work with. Experience tells me that working with people who share a similar view of the world is so much more rewarding in every sense than working with those who do not.

> **Short-term vs. Long-term**
> Some clients can offer you an immediate financial return, while others can offer you the chance to build your reputation and experience, and assist in the growth of your business over a longer period of time.

Greater certainty and conviction to say 'no'

The principle of saying no must be ruthlessly applied if you are to be successful. Working with anyone other than your ideal client and attending events dominated by less than ideal clients will distract you from achieving your goals. By compromising, you take yourself further away from becoming the business or organisation you want to be and you may find yourself resenting the work you are undertaking.

> *The more time you spend on clients who are not right for you, the less time you have to spend on finding those who are.*

Where there is an invitation to speak at a conference outside your key industry sector, clarity regarding your ideal client will enable you to quickly establish that the opportunity, while flattering, is not the right one for you to achieve your goals. The last thing you want to be doing with your limited time is fielding calls from people who heard you speak, but who are not right for your business or organisation.

If you're running your own business, having the conviction to say no takes on even greater relevance. Running your own business allows you to dictate who you work with and the type of work you undertake. Working with anyone except those you really want to work with is wasting the opportunity and benefit of self-employment.

There are three exceptions to this principle:

1. When you practise a skill or test a new product on an audience that are not your ideal clients.

2. If someone approaches you and therefore there has been no cost to acquire the business you may decide to take the revenue on offer if that revenue is of use to you at that time, e.g. 'It's not my ideal client but we do have free time in the schedule and it will pay for the new website.'

3. Economic conditions may dictate the necessity to take a piece of business that is not your ideal to fill a revenue gap.

The key in all cases is to be aware of the reasons you take any revenue and be very, very selective – these are very much exceptions, not the rule.

One of the industry sectors I provide training to is the exhibition industry. Whilst there is great pressure to sell exhibition space on shows, they have to ensure that they get the right exhibitors to buy space. If they don't, they end up with an exhibition that does not appeal to the visitors.

Similarly if they don't attract the right visitors, this can create a negative experience for the exhibitors. Clarity of ideal exhibitor and ideal visitor is crucial to the long term viability of the exhibition.

KEY POINTS

- Developing clarity on who you want to work with – your ideal client – is the starting point for success in business development

- Saying no to people and opportunities that do not represent your ideal client is essential to your success

EXERCISES

- Identify which of your existing clients you want to do more business with. Why?

- Identify which of your existing clients you want to do less business with. Why?

- Develop a clear mental picture of your ideal client

- Remind yourself who your ideal client is every day

Notes

2 | DEVELOPING YOUR PROPOSITION

Once you have identified your ideal client, you need a compelling and relevant proposition that speaks directly to them. Your proposition should be clear and strong enough that when your ideal client hears or reads it, he is left in no doubt that he needs to engage with you.

Imagine your ideal clients are standing at a bus stop. When your bus comes along, they should be in no doubt that yours is the one they need to catch to get them to where they want to go.

A mistake often made is to have a proposition that is too general and consequently attracts no one. For example, if a business was to say that it delivered coaching this could be open to various interpretations, for example business coaching, career coaching, sports coaching or voice coaching.

A strong, compelling proposition is required to attract the people you want to do business with.

A strong proposition will ensure that your clients aren't left standing at the bus stop when your bus goes past.

How to develop a compelling proposition

A strong proposition answers the following questions:

- Audience – who is your ideal client?

- Need – what is your ideal client's burning issue that you can address?

- Solution – what outcomes can you deliver?

- Proof – what evidence do you have?

- Point of difference – what differentiates you from your competitors?

Your proposition should speak directly to your ideal client.

If you can clearly articulate your answers to these questions, in verbal and written communication, you will be more effective at attracting business.

Communicating your proposition verbally

At business and social events, when people ask you, 'What do you do?', you have the opportunity to attract your ideal clients by using your verbal proposition, also known as your elevator pitch.

The length of your response will vary depending on the specific situation. Some situations call for a brief response while others may call for a longer description.

Here is an example of a verbal proposition that could be used at a business or social event to provide an initial, concise response to the 'What do you do?' question. Observe how each statement builds on the opportunity to attract an ideal client.

If time permits, each of these points can be expanded as the conversation develops.

Example

Personal introduction
My name is John Smith
Organisation
I'm from Memorable Amazing Events
Who uses your product (audience)
We work with fast-moving consumer goods companies
Burning issues you address (need)
To help them successfully launch their brands
Outcomes (solution)
We design launches that announce a brand's arrival in the marketplace and kick-starts engagement with its audience
Proof
Our recent jobs have included launches for ABC Consumer Goods and Consolidated Goods Inc. Both launches generated over one million dollars in positive media coverage for our clients
What makes you different from your competitors
We work exclusively with fast-moving consumer goods companies, which means that our clients can draw upon our wealth of industry experience relevant to their needs

We want the reaction from our ideal client to be:

I need to speak to John. He has demonstrated how his company has helped other organisations with similar needs to ours achieve great outcomes.

When you start to use your elevator pitch on your ideal clients, be aware which phrases people respond to positively. Make a note of these phrases and keep refining your pitch until you have something that you feel comfortable with and that creates interest. What you end up with may not follow the exact sequence in the example, but should cover the key elements.

It may take some time to develop an elevator pitch that you feel good about. Once you do, it will turn networking events into something to look forward to, rather than avoid.

Communicating your proposition in writing

Your proposition will also be used in written communication such as sales collateral, emails, letters and on your website. Done correctly, when people land on your homepage they will know immediately they have found an organisation that can address their needs. If your proposition is not communicated effectively, they will click away from your page immediately. The same principle applies in sales collateral, presentations, emails and letters to engage prospects.

In all cases we want our ideal clients to think:

I need to speak to these people.

Briefer versions can also be used on business cards and email signatures, e.g. 'Helping fast moving consumer goods companies successfully launch new brands.'

More than one proposition

It is possible to develop more than one proposition to target various ideal clients. You could develop an overall broad proposition and then tailor it to target specific segments.

My experience

I use language that talks in terms of my client's needs rather than the services I deliver. For example, if I say that *I help organisations to become more effective at attracting clients, customers, sponsors and funding,* I am much more likely to create interest and attract my ideal clients than if I used a tired old phrase like *I provide training and consulting.*

When meeting potential corporate partners at networking events, representatives of charities when asked 'what they do' will too often simply reply that they 'work for a charity'. This may make the person that asked the question think that you are a caring person but it will not necessarily move them any closer to developing a business relationship with your organisation.

A more beneficial response would be to say that you work for a charity and your role is to work with companies to help them demonstrate their brand values, inspire their staff and project a positive image in the community. As these are all typical outcomes desired by a company, this will invariably lead to the opportunity to discuss further the work you do at the charity and to explore the corporate's specific needs.

KEY POINTS

- Developing a clear and concise proposition gives you the opportunity to attract your ideal clients

- Constantly develop and fine tune your elevator pitch

EXERCISES

- Prepare your elevator pitch

- Practise your elevator pitch on colleagues or friends. Does your proposition make sense? Could it be stronger? Do you feel comfortable saying it?

- Review your proposition on your website homepage and other written communication to ensure it speaks clearly and directly to your audience

Notes

3 | FINDING PROSPECTS

Now that you have identified who you want to do business with – your ideal clients – and your proposition to attract them, you need an effective business development activity plan that outlines exactly where you will find these new clients.

Your plan should outline, month by month, the activities that will enable you to identify and attract sufficient numbers of prospects to convert into clients and thereby achieve your targets based on your sales pipeline ratios.

Be realistic

Your business development activity plan must be realistic in the sense that the activities proposed are ones that you are able and willing to implement.

Be robust

Your plan must be robust. You must be able to look at your plan and say, 'If I implement this plan, based on my current prospect-to-client conversion rate and my knowledge of how to identify and attract my ideal clients, I will achieve my targets.' If you implement a weak plan, you won't achieve your targets.

Put it in writing

Write your plan down. If you don't commit to a written plan to undertake a required amount of business development activity, you'll stay busy dealing with your existing clients while the weeks and months pass by. I have heard this excuse many times!

SALES PIPELINE

The sales pipeline places prospects at different stages of the sales process and measures their progress through the pipeline from unqualified prospect through to client. For example, you may need to meet with five different companies to convert one new client. To meet with five different companies you may have needed to approach twenty qualified prospects and to find twenty qualified prospects you may have needed to identify thirty prospects. You will need to undertake sufficient activity to identify thirty prospects at the start. This is where the business development activity plan comes in to ensure that identification of the required number of prospects is achieved. Remember: These numbers vary from industry to industry.

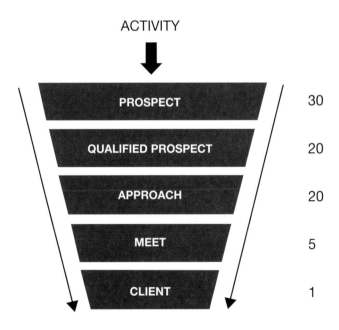

ACTIVITY

PROSPECT	30
QUALIFIED PROSPECT	20
APPROACH	20
MEET	5
CLIENT	1

Key components of a plan

There are four key components to a robust business development activity plan:

1. Targets
2. Activities
3. Timing
4. Prospect-to-client conversion rates

1. Targets

The starting point in your plan is establishing quantifiable targets. Targets are typically expressed in terms of the desired number of clients and amount of revenue in a given time period, usually a year.

2. Activities

Next, your plan should outline the activities you will undertake to identify prospects to approach as well as to attract prospects to you. Identifying prospects to approach and attracting prospects to you are two separate, yet complementary methods of developing business.

Activity is crucial. One of the key reasons people don't achieve their targets is failure to undertake enough of the right kind of activity. This leads to a lack of prospects to convert to clients based on their conversion rates. Too often people undertake too much of the wrong kinds of activity, repeating the same ineffective approach time and time again.

I recommend that you break your activity into the following categories:

- Prospect identification activities in personal channels
- Prospect identification activities in non-personal channels
- Marketing activities
- Attraction activities

Prospect identification activities in personal channels

Personal relationships are a key part of the business development process. Identify places you can go to meet prospects – your potential ideal clients – face-to-face, such as conferences, and networking and social events. This will bring you face to face not only with known prospects but also with prospects that up to that point you were unaware of – the process increases your prospect universe. A good technique is to ask your ideal clients which business and personal events they attend – this will give you clues regarding how to find more of the people you are looking to attract.

If you establish and nurture a relationship with prospects, it gives you permission to contact them (avoiding the cold call), and when they need to buy, they are more likely to buy from you. Too often relationships are sought at the point when sales are required – this is too late. In my experience, if you focus on building relationships, the sales will take care of themselves.

This approach may not deliver immediate results, however a year down the track when you have established five new relationships each month – 60 new relationships in a year – you will be thankful that you made the effort.

Prospect identification activities in non-personal channels

Identify relevant industry specific and broader based media within channels such as television, magazines, websites and newspapers and read and view them daily, weekly and monthly to identify new prospects. Look out for who is active in marketing.

Look at their target audience, their message and their positioning, This will give you ideas for prospects. Identify companies that are going through change such as merging, re-branding, launching new products and introducing new management. It's at these times they may require new suppliers or there may be a chance for you to replace the incumbent supplier.

Developing habits

In the case of both personal and non-personal channels, the key is to develop the habit of attending events as well as reading and viewing relevant media. If you attend events where your ideal clients are present and your competitors are not, and if you use your elevator pitch successfully, you – not your competitor – will attract your ideal client. If you view relevant media and your competitors do not, all things being equal, you – not your competitor – will identify your next prospect.

Marketing activities

Outline traditional marketing activities, such as advertising, direct marketing and public relations, as well as new forms of marketing, such as regular use of social media and Search Engine Optimisation (SEO).

Attraction activities

Outline the activities that will allow your ideal client to experience you and your organisation, product or service in action. For example, accept opportunities to speak at industry events or host your own event. Attraction activities are, in my observation, the most powerful of all marketing activities. (For further information on attracting prospects, see Chapter 6.)

3. Timing

Identify which activities you plan to undertake month by month, which activities you plan to undertake week by week and which activities you plan to undertake day by day. Timelines act as accountable deadlines and are fundamental to success.

4. Prospect-to-client conversion rates

Finally, based on your own experience of what works for you in business development and your conversion rates, outline the anticipated number of prospects, meetings and clients to be generated through each activity and channel. For example, you may anticipate that you will need to find thirty qualified prospects in personal channels to generate twenty meetings to convert ten clients, as shown in the table below.

Activities	Prospects	Meetings	Clients
Personal channels	30 ⇨	20 ⇨	10
Non-personal channels	60	25	10
Marketing activities	60	25	10
Attraction activities	20	15	10
Total	**170**	**85**	**40**

The ratios suggested here reflect that attraction activities and personal channels are the most effective and efficient ways of generating business. This is because these channels enable people to experi-

Your targets drive your activity and your activity drives your sales.

ence you. The power of experience can be so strong that a prospect may decide to purchase from you or use your organisation even before you have finished speaking or demonstrating your product. Remember, these figures are examples only and ratios will vary from person to person and industry to industry.

By taking this approach, you will have a robust, realistic and written plan of activity to achieve your targets based on your personal conversion rates. It is the actual activity you now undertake that will determine whether or not you successfully achieve your targets. A template plan has been included on the following page.

While the dollar-revenue target for a year could be the same for two different businesses, the number of clients required to meet the target may be vastly different. For example, a business selling high-value software needs only two clients at $500,000 each to reach its $1 million annual target. However, a business selling exhibition space may need 100 exhibitors at an average sale price of $10,000 each to achieve the same annual revenue target.

Business Development Activity Plan

Channel/ activity	Prospects or Leads	Meeting	Clients	JAN	FEB	MAR	APR	MAY	JUN	JUL	AUG	SEP	OCT	NOV	DEC
Personal															
Non-personal															
Marketing															
Attraction															
TOTAL															

MOMENTUM-BUILDING ACTIVITIES

Effective business development is all about ensuring that you undertake activities that build momentum in your sales effort and propel you towards achieving your targets. A realistic and robust written business development activity plan will ensure that this happens. To get momentum, you have to put in a concerted effort at the start and sometimes you need the right support to help you achieve it. But like a snowball that grows as it gathers pace, once you get momentum, business development takes on a life of its own.

Momentum gives you results, results give you confidence – and confidence gives you more momentum.

Activity is key!

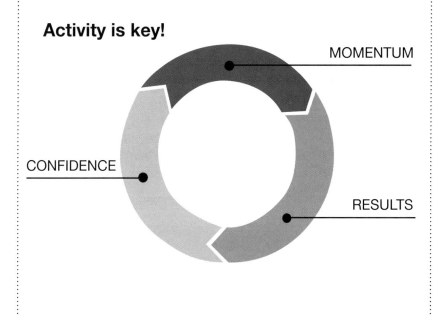

Effort leads to reward

When I put in a concerted, focused effort to attract my ideal clients through activities such as speaking at conferences, the return – although often not immediate – is always worth the initial effort multiplied many times.

Persevere

People fail not only because they lack a robust plan and don't put in the required effort: they fail because they stop just before they get momentum. They expect returns from their efforts to be immediate and, when they don't experience them, they wrongly conclude that the activity was not worthwhile. In a business to business environment with long lead times this thinking is naive.

The key is to identify and undertake activities that you know are right for you to undertake, even if they don't provide an immediate return, and track their success over time.

KEY POINTS

- Your future clients and success are determined by the activities you undertake today

- Develop a realistic, written and robust business development activity plan that outlines exactly where you can find prospective clients. With consistent effort behind it, your plan will give you the momentum to achieve your targets

EXERCISES

- Write a business development activity plan for the year ahead. Clarify your targets and decide:

  - What momentum-building activities you are going to undertake

  - Where you are going to go to meet your ideal clients

  - What you are going to read and view to identify prospects to approach

  - What marketing activities you are going to undertake

  - What attraction activities you are going to undertake (For further information on attraction activities, see Chapter 6.)

Notes

4

REFINING PROSPECTS

Having implemented your business development activity plan, you will generate a list of new prospects to add to those that you may already have. Before approaching any of the prospects on your list you must first segment, declutter and refine the list.

Prospect lists and segmentation

One of the biggest mistakes people make is to approach everyone on their prospect list – qualified and unqualified prospects alike – using the same method without considering their attractiveness in terms of the potential return to their organisation. People often spend valuable time approaching unqualified prospects, and not enough time researching and preparing to successfully engage more attractive prospects. By not undertaking enough research and preparation you may blow your one, and often only, chance to impress your qualified prospects.

The solution to identifying the best prospects is to segment your list in terms of attractiveness. Then you can take the time to cultivate relationships and engage the most attractive prospects in a manner that will reflect their potential return and gives you the best chance of successfully engaging with them.

Prospect lists and clutter

Too many prospect lists contain a large number of out-of-date prospects. A long prospect list gives the illusion of an abundance of future clients when, in reality, the list of hot prospects is not as long or as hot as you think. The key is to declutter your prospect list.

Imagine your prospect list is like a wardrobe packed with out-of-date items of clothing that you should have got rid of a long time ago. Those old clothes stop you from seeing what is useful to you right now and in the future.

Decluttering enables you to identify prospects that have real potential, and to define the amount of new business development activity required to fill your pipeline. Get rid of those prospects where no action has taken place and no action will be undertaken. Like those old jeans you haven't worn for years, let those prospects go.

Be ruthless – your future success is determined by the quality and quantity of today's prospect list. Don't be satisfied until you have an up-to-date prospect list large enough to achieve your targets based on your conversion rates.

Create a list outlining:

- The name of each prospect

- The reason they are a prospect

- The specific action to be undertaken

- Who is responsible for undertaking the action

- When the action will be done

Prospect research

Once you have followed the steps above you will be left with a refined prospect list which you now need to research. Research is key to developing a successful approach. The more attractive the prospect, the more research is required. Good business development practice is knowing what makes your prospect tick.

Here are three questions you need to answer before you approach any prospect:

1. Do you understand your prospect's business hot buttons?

2. Do you understand your prospect's personal hot buttons?

3. Have you developed ideas around how you can help your prospect's business?

If you haven't established the answers to these questions, don't approach the prospect yet. You only have one chance to make the all-important first impression. You don't want to blow it because you didn't do your research.

1. Identifying your prospect's business hot buttons

Your prospect's hot buttons are the key business issues, challenges and needs your prospect is facing. A great way to identify these is to experience their brand. For example, if you are approaching a car company, take a trip to the local dealership and talk to the sales team about their challenges. Look at what models are coming out, find out what audiences are being targeted and look at what themes are being used in advertising and promotions.

2. Identifying your prospect's personal hot buttons

Develop knowledge about the people who work in the business you are going to approach and identify their hot buttons. Research their role in the company, their responsibilities, experience and interests. For example, if you know that your prospect's background and role is in human resources, it may help when you approach them to emphasise how your opportunity will benefit the people in their organisation. Similarly, if your prospect's background is in sales, emphasise the impact on sales; if they are in finance, emphasise the bottom line; and if they are in marketing, emphasise the contribution your organisation can make to their brand and marketing campaign. I find Google and LinkedIn are useful tools for this kind of research.

3. Developing ideas around how you can help your prospect

This is the solution you can provide to help them address their challenges and needs. For example, if you identify that a car company is launching a new model at the same time as you are holding an event that will attract a similar audience, you can suggest to them that they utilise your event to accelerate the awareness and understanding of the new model through publicity, branding, display space and promotions.

Tailor your approach

By answering the three questions you have about your prospects – what their business and personal hot buttons are, and how can you help their organisation – you can construct a relevant approach that will engage the prospect in their own world. By placing your prospect's issues and language at the centre of your communication, you will increase your chances of getting the prospect to engage with you.

KEY POINTS

- Your future success is determined by the quality and quantity of your prospect list, and the research you undertake today

- The more information you can find on the business and personal hot buttons of your prospect, the more you can tailor an approach that is likely to result in positive outcomes

EXERCISES

- Segment and declutter your prospect list

- Before making an approach to a prospect, undertake detailed research to establish their personal and business hot buttons and develop a concept of how you can help them to address their needs

Notes

5 | APPROACHING PROSPECTS

Now that you have refined your prospect list, researched your prospects' business and personal hot buttons and developed a concept for helping them, you are ready to make the approach.

In approaching prospects, you have to balance approaching a sufficient number of prospects to achieve your pipeline targets with ensuring that every approach is tailored to give you the best chance of successfully engaging the prospect.

The reason people are often unsuccessful is simply that they don't approach enough prospects to achieve their sales pipeline ratios – some people spend too much time on preparation without getting on with prospect engagement. Others approach too many prospects in a generic fashion without consideration of the needs and challenges of that specific organisation. Consequently they receive multiple objections. A participant at one of my workshops told me she had sent out fifty letters to prospects and received not one positive response. 'What did you do next?' I inquired. 'I sent out fifty more,' she replied. I wondered how many more letters would have to be sent out before the light came on that a different, more considered approach might be more productive. The correct balance of quantity and quality in your approaches is the 'sweet spot' of activity.

Methods of approach

The key methods of approaching a prospect are through:

- Personal contact
- Cold calling on the telephone or in writing
- Something more creative

Personal contact

One of the biggest obstacles people find in business development is getting to speak to the right person in a prospect company. Having a personal contact within your prospect organisation is by far the best method of gaining traction. That is why it is important to:

- Spend time mapping out all potential connections into your prospect company

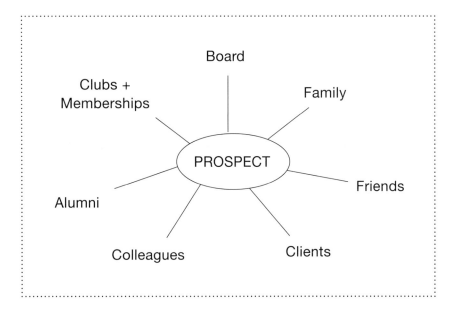

- Get into the habit of actively socialising and networking to build your own extensive body of relationships

- Use your connections' connections – ask board members, colleagues or friends to introduce you to prospects. Note – board members are more likely to provide you with access to their contacts if you speak to them one-on-one not as a group

- Develop a plan to attract well-connected people of influence and persuasion to your organisation – such as charities having high profile ambassadors and board members

Cold calling on the telephone or in writing

If you don't have the luxury of an introduction or a personal relationship with your prospect, you may have to cold call. This may be from an existing list, a purchased list or a list you have developed from your own research. Whether you use the telephone, send a letter through the post or make contact on line, there are several key principles to successfully approach prospects and turn your call from cold to warm:

- Need – demonstrate an understanding of their business and their need

- Solution – whet their appetite on how you can provide a solution to their need

- Proof – demonstrate credibility of how you have helped others in a similar situation

- Next step – outline what you want

The following examples can be tailored for use on the phone or in a letter or email.

- Need: Demonstrate an understanding of their business and their need.

  I read in Marketing Magazine you are launching a new brand in September targeting the fitness industry.

- Solution: Whet their appetite on how you can provide a solution to their need.

  My reason for contacting you is that our fitness industry exhibition is taking place in September. The event attracts 10,000 representatives from the industry who come together once a year over three days in one location to explore and experience the latest industry products and services. This event would be an ideal opportunity to drive awareness and understanding of your new brand and accelerate cut-through among your target audience.

- Proof: Demonstrate credibility of how you have helped someone else in a similar situation.

  We recently helped ABCD Fitness Products Company to successfully launch its new brand capturing a 25% market share in the first six months.

- Next step: Outline what you want. In this scenario, we want a face-to-face meeting.

  I would like to set up a brief meeting with you to discuss ways we can help you to launch your brand to our audience.

The key to successful cold calling is to ensure that you:

1. Focus your communication on the outcomes you can deliver for your prospect

Focus on the outcomes your prospect will benefit from as a result of their involvement with you. Talk less about what you do and more about what the prospect will get from you. Outline the positive things you can give them, such as increased brand awareness, customer retention and loyalty, higher sales, greater efficiencies and positive customer and/or employee relationships. You may also want to outline the negative things you can help reduce, such as employee turnover, overhead costs and laborious waiting times. Quantify your statements with examples wherever possible.

2. Use their language

Use language from their world, not yours. People are more likely to engage with you when you have a shared understanding and commonality of language.

3. Talk benefits, not just features

Approach your prospect not only with the features you can offer their organisation, but the benefits they will reap from these features. For instance, rather than say, *We run the events in fifteen countries*, tell them what the benefit is: *We run the events in fifteen countries, which means that we can provide you with a platform to launch your brand globally.*

Similarly, rather than say, *We have offices in Sydney, New York and London,* tell them what the benefit is: *We have offices in Sydney, New York and London, which means that you will have real-time access twenty four hours a day to our team to deal with your requirements as and when they occur.*

4. Get to the point

The mistake people make when writing to new prospects is sending written material that is too long, visually uninviting, contains too much narrative and is devoid of key messages. Similar mistakes can be made over the phone. Keep your message short and to the point. (For more information on key messages see Chapter 11.)

Using the telephone

The telephone is an unforgiving vehicle for communication as you only have a brief chance – approximately thirty seconds – to make a positive first impression. Like many aspects of the business development process, preparation can dramatically enhance your chance of successfully cold-calling a prospect on the telephone.

The following will help you prepare:

1. Physical location

Ensure that your physical location is conducive to having a productive conversation with your prospect. Ideally, you want a quiet location with no background noise or interruptions. If you are in a busy open-plan office, consider using a meeting room to make those important calls.

2. Frame of mind

Going into the phone call with a positive frame of mind is essential. If you are not in the right frame of mind, hold that call! A useful technique for getting into a positive state of mind is to recall a previous phone conversation with a prospect that went well and to reassociate with the positive feelings from that experience. Also visualise your next call: feel, hear and see yourself speaking in a confident, friendly, engaging, professional and assertive manner, with the prospect responding positively to your pitch.

3. Clear objectives

Be clear on the objective of your call. If you provide a service or solution requiring a large degree of financial commitment, it is unlikely that the prospect will buy over the phone. The objective of the call is to get a meeting. Once a meeting has been agreed to, end the call and start preparing for the meeting.

4. Objections

Think through your prospect's potential objections and your responses in advance. You'll be thankful you took the time to prepare when you expertly respond to their concerns.

5. Pen and paper ready

Have pen and paper ready to capture the key points of the conversation. Writing down the key points under discussion eliminates the quandary later on in the day when you can't remember all the points your prospect made.

6. Practise the call

Practise the call in advance through role-play. Role-playing will give you insights on how to improve the real call.

7. Research

Ensure that you have undertaken enough research on the

prospect you are about to cold call to help you have a meaningful conversation with them.

8. Structure

Ensure that you have planned the key elements of your call, known as the *conversational milestones.* Conversational milestones should include:

- Informing the prospect of the purpose of your call

- Demonstrating to the prospect that you have done your homework about their organisation

- Creating interest for the prospect – what's in it for them

- Outlining what you want to happen next

9. Delivery

Adapt the volume, tone, pace and emphasis in your voice to match that of your prospect. Listen for clues that can tell you what state of mind your prospect is in at that moment. For example, do you hear someone requiring information immediately or someone who has time to talk? For successful engagement with your prospect, you should respond to what you hear and adapt your delivery accordingly.

10. Scripts

Never read from a script as it will sound…like you are reading from a script! Instead, prepare and outline the conversational milestones you want to cover in your call.

Creative approach

In my observation, too many people are too quick to pick up the phone and write letters without considering whether that method is the most effective way of engaging potential clients. At worst, people churn through their prospect list leaving a negative impression in their wake. By a creative approach, I am referring to initiatives like sending a physical item that attracts your prospect's attention, creates interest and acts as a conversation starter when you call them. For example, if you are targeting a key sponsor for an event which has a keynote speaker, you might send a copy of your keynote speaker's book with a letter informing them that you will be calling them next week to discuss an opportunity that will allow them to drive awareness of their brand and engage key decision-makers in their industry sector. Similarly, if you were selling shirt sponsorship for a football team you could mock up the shirt with the prospect's logo on it. If you are selling services to a specific industry, you could send them a report on trends within the industry, or your views on emerging issues.

By taking a more considered approach that provides the opportunity to engage in dialogue and build relationships with your prospects, you will increase your success rate and your enjoyment of the whole process.

KEY POINT

- The key to successfully approaching a prospect is to tailor your content and delivery to the world of the prospect and to focus on the relevant outcomes you can deliver for them

EXERCISES

- Develop a letter to a prospect that encapsulates the key principles of an effective approach

- Before calling any prospect, ensure that you have planned for, and practised, an effective phone call

- Develop a creative technique that provides an opportunity for dialogue with a prospect

Notes

Notes

6 | ATTRACTING PROSPECTS

If your approach to developing new business is limited to identifying and approaching prospects, you will miss out on the most effective marketing tool of all: attraction.

What is attraction marketing?

Attraction comes from undertaking activities that allow your ideal clients to *experience* you from a personal and business perspective. Rather than telling your prospects how great you are, you *demonstrate* your credentials. Attraction is based on the concepts that *people prefer to work with people they like and trust,* those who *share a similar view of the world*, and with businesses that can *solve their problems.*

Experience

By getting your ideal client to experience you from a personal and business perspective, you provide an opportunity to create an emotional and logical connection far stronger than any testimonial, or marketing message about your product or service. When your audience experiences you, they get a sense of the real you and your approach. Those who like your approach and share your view of the world will be attracted to you – and those people who don't, won't.

Demonstration

Anyone can claim to have certain attributes. You need to differentiate yourself from your competitors by demonstrating, rather than claiming, your expertise. Demonstrating your expertise eliminates the need to claim anything – a good comedian doesn't need to claim that they make people laugh.

I like what she says and the way that she says it. These are the people for us.

Attraction in action

In order for prospects to experience you demonstrating your credentials, you need to implement an attraction strategy. Attraction strategies include:

- Speaking at events where your prospects are present – identify relevant events and put yourself forward as a speaker

- Writing articles for publications or recording videos for websites that your prospects will read and view – approach relevant media to discuss providing articles and videos

- Inviting prospects to an event or performance so they can experience the features and benefits you have on offer while building relationships. For example, when I was marketing manager at KPMG, we would invite prospects and clients to a post budget breakfast which allowed us to demonstrate our expertise regarding tax and, having met a prospect, it provided a greater opportunity to set up a time to meet to talk about their specific taxation needs. A number of my arts clients invite prospects to experience a performance and the potential features and benefits they could access through a partnership. This also aids the relationship-building process.

In all cases, the key is to:

- Talk to your prospect about the issues they are facing – Need

- Show ways you can assist them to overcome their issues – Solution

Need +
Solution + Proof
= Success

- Demonstrate how you have helped other people in a similar situation to achieve similar outcomes – Proof

My experience

In my personal experience, the most effective method of developing business is by attraction, through speaking and writing. I find it both enjoyable and rewarding.

One example is when I teamed up with a recruitment agency who invited their clients and prospects in one of the sectors they recruit in to hear me speak about business development. Fifty-three people turned up and at the end the CEO from one of the organisations present asked to me work with her team to help them double their revenue over the next six years. The people and the organisation fitted exactly my ideal client profile; a progressive, dynamic organisation undertaking great work with a great team of people who are fun to work with and committed to improvement. Did I approach them? No, they approached me – that's the power of attraction marketing. And in addition, a number of other participants went on to attend my public workshops. The recruitment agency and I are now undertaking similar talks with different industry sectors.

The benefits of an attraction strategy

- **Time efficient, with positive reinforcement**

Speaking to 100 people at an event is like undertaking 100 sales calls in 45 minutes. Those who like what you say will approach you after the event and people will leave with a positive impression of you. This is a very different experience to approaching 100 people by phone or by letter where you potentially receive a large number of knock-backs just to get a small number of people to meet with you.

- **You expand your prospect universe**

When you undertake activities such as speaking and writing, you can engage and attract businesses you may never have heard of. While your competitors are approaching known prospects, you're flushing out new ideal clients you would have never considered approaching – because you were not aware they existed.

- **No need to sell: talk and write**

For people uncomfortable with the idea of selling, the good news is that you don't have to cold call ever again. Talk about, write about and demonstrate your products and services to your ideal clients whenever you have the opportunity and you will attract your ideal clients to you.

- **You stand out**

There may be hundreds of people offering what you offer, but by demonstrating your credentials you stand out from the crowd and YOU get noticed. In today's world, we don't always have time to research and consider all the possible options. If you have a need and you have just experienced someone who can help satisfy that need, why would you look elsewhere?

- **Quality, qualified prospects**

From my observation, when you use attraction strategies that allow you to demonstrate your credentials, and your ideal clients to experience you, you always attract higher quality prospects – prospects that are right for you.

If you fail to attract your ideal clients

If your ideal clients experience you and this does not generate business for you, something is wrong in your approach. Stop your attraction activities until this is resolved. The problem may be to do with the relevance of your product or service in meeting their needs, the way that you communicate the features and benefits, or how you come across as a person. Whatever it is, you need to identify it and change it because there is no point attempting to engage prospects again until you do.

KEY POINT

- Attraction activities are a powerful way of drawing the right prospects to you. Attraction activities provide the opportunity to *demonstrate* your expertise and for your ideal clients to *experience* you.

EXERCISES

- Identify attraction activities you can undertake that will allow your audience to experience you and what you have to offer

- Identify events your audience will be attending over the next year and put yourself forward as a speaker

- Identify what your audience will be reading over the next 12 months and put yourself forward to write articles in the relevant publications

- Review all of your communication for opportunities to demonstrate your expertise, rather than tell people how good you are

Notes

Notes

7 | PREPARING FOR A SALES MEETING

Once you have successfully approached or attracted your prospect, it's time to prepare for the first meeting.

As I am sure you know, obtaining a meeting with a prospect can sometimes be a challenge. So given the opportunity to finally meet your prospect, you have to make the most of the opportunity. Here are some key actions you can undertake to prepare for your next prospect sales meeting that will enhance your chance of success. I have broken the actions down into themes.

People

- Establish who will be attending the meeting on your prospect's side.

- Find out their job title and role within the organisation. This will allow you to focus the conversation on each person's specific area of interest. For example, you may want to discuss the challenges of managing people with the human resources manager, or the challenges inherent in sales with the sales manager.

- Research each person's background to find out about their education, life experiences and interests. This will help you to build rapport at a content level by introducing shared reference points into the conversation.

- Determine who you will take to the meeting. Take along the people that will actually do the work and let them speak about what they will do. This will give the prospect confidence that what you promise will be delivered.

A business developer in a professional services firm told me how she had not won a job because a competing firm had taken a team of people to the presentation whilst she had gone on her own. The team's presence had given the prospect confidence that the work would be delivered.

Your prospect's business

- Identify current issues facing your prospect's business.

- Identify current trends within your prospect's industry.

Doing both will demonstrate that you have done your homework on their business and will enable you to have a meaningful conversation around their challenges.

- Consider the cultural norms, dress and language used within the prospect's organisation. Matching each allows you to build a rapport through non-verbal as well as verbal communication.

Objectives

- Identify the information you want to obtain from the meeting.

- Determine your desired outcome for the meeting. Are you expecting a sale then and there, or permission to come back and present a fully costed proposal? Decide on your meeting objective.

Process

- Establish your process, or sequence of activity, for the meeting. For instance, you may plan your conversation around first building rapport, then uncovering the prospect's needs, exploring solutions to their issues and agreeing to the next steps.

- If you are with a colleague, determine the role each of you will play in the meeting.

Questions

- Outline in advance questions that will help start the discussion.

- Prepare answers to questions that you might be asked.

- Prepare responses to potential objections that might be raised.

- If you are with a colleague, determine who will answer each question and/or respond to each objection.

Time

- Confirm the meeting the day before, as well as the meeting duration.

- Agree on an agenda with your prospect beforehand.

Logistics

- Ensure you know the exact location of the meeting, how to get there and how long it will take to get there.

- Confirm what technology will be available and have a plan B if the technology fails.

- Ensure you have enough business cards to distribute to the attendees.

Mindset

- Visualise: see, hear and feel how you want the meeting to play out.

- Play a quick burst of your favourite music to yourself before the meeting to enhance your mood.

Both techniques will help you to create a positive mindset and pre-program your subconscious mind towards a positive desired outcome. (For more information on mindset, see Chapter 14.)

KEY POINT

- Preparing for a meeting will greatly enhance your success in the meeting

EXERCISE

- Ensure all the actions listed above are applied in advance of your next meeting and give yourself the best chance for a successful sales meeting with your prospect

Notes

8 | BUILDING RAPPORT

Having secured a meeting with your prospect, the meeting will now consist of four key stages. These are:

1. Building rapport
2. Uncovering needs
3. Exploring solutions
4. Agreeing next steps

Building rapport with your prospect is the foundation for a fruitful relationship – and relationships are integral to success in business development.

What is 'rapport'?

People often think of rapport as simply the ability to interact socially with people. While skills in social interaction are essential in business, rapport is a deeper level of trust and understanding between two or more people.

Why is rapport important?

People prefer to do business with people they like, trust and feel comfortable with. If a prospect trusts you, you have greater opportunity to influence their thinking and behaviour. A prospect who likes you is more likely to share information with you. This will allow you to provide a tailored and unique solution to meet his or her needs.

The bigger the risk in terms of financial commitment, the greater the degree of trust required. For instance, if you approach a prospect to sell them a $1 raffle ticket, a minimal level of trust is necessary. But if you approach a prospect with a million dollar deal, significantly more trust is required.

How to build rapport

Rapport often occurs naturally – I am sure we have all met people with whom we seem to 'click' straightaway. However, when rapport is not present, we have to create it. You build rapport by joining the other person's world.

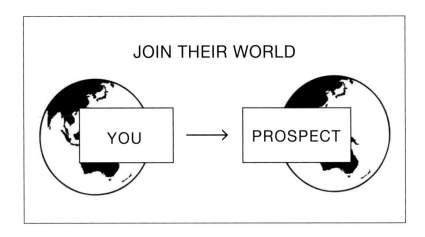

Here are four ways to join your prospect's world:

1. Content

Build rapport at a content level by talking to your prospect about their business challenges and personal interests using their words, phrases, terminology and language rather than yours. Mutual reference points are also good for building rapport, such as mutual contacts, interest and backgrounds. Research is important, as it allows you to have a meaningful conversation with the prospect in his or her world. For example, if your research shows that a prospect has recently undertaken a new marketing campaign, engage them in conversation about how the campaign is going.

2. Questions

Asking questions not only engages the prospect in the content of his or her world, it shows a genuine desire and interest to understand your prospect. (For more information on questioning technique, see Chapter 9.)

3. Dress

Dress is an instant visual cue. As soon as we meet someone, we form a view of them based on what they are wearing. The key to building rapport at a visual level is to dress for the world of your prospect, without compromising yourself and what you stand for.

Many sales approaches fail because people stay inside their own world, talking enthusiastically about their organisation and what they have to offer, rather than taking the time to participate in and understand the world of the prospect they are trying to attract.

4. Verbal and non-verbal communication

People in rapport with one another will match each other's postures, gestures, vocal tone and intonation. Even their breathing may synchronise. By observing this level of communication between yourself and your prospect and matching your prospect's verbal and non-verbal communication, you can establish another way to build rapport.

In my experience, I am very aware of the culturally different environments of my clients. For example, when I deal with certain football codes, people commonly use the word 'mate' in conversation. This is quite different from the language used in arts organisations. Using the wrong language in the wrong environment can break rapport.

Take time to build rapport

It is important to take time to build rapport at the start of a meeting. Prepare questions from your research to ask the prospect and put them at ease. The length of time given to building rapport will vary from person to person and meeting to meeting.

The key is to recognise what is going on for the person in front of you and respond accordingly.

If a prospect gives the impression they are busy and wants to get straight down to business, get to the 'what's in it for them' pretty quickly. If they want to spend a while talking about sport, talk away. When you do get a sense from their verbal and non-verbal cues that the rapport-building phase is coming to an end and they want to move on, use a bridging question to move the conversation to the uncovering needs phase, such as:

Thanks for agreeing to see us today. As you know, we are here to talk to you about an opportunity that we believe could help you successfully launch your new brand. I'd like to start by asking you one or two questions about your plans for the launch and the outcomes you are looking to achieve.

*It's about where **they** are at, not where **you** are at.*

Then move into the questioning phase. (For more information on this phase, see Chapter 9.)

KEY POINTS

- Take the time to build rapport. It will help you to develop trust and understanding with your prospect

- Build rapport by 'joining the world' of your prospect

EXERCISES

- Undertake research on your prospect – both the person and the business – that will allow you to build rapport at a content level by asking meaningful questions at your next meeting

- Observe the body language of your colleagues in meetings. What do your observations tell you?

Notes

9 | UNCOVERING NEEDS

Once you have built rapport with your prospect, you now move on to the most important part of the entire business development process: uncovering your prospect's needs.

Uncovering your prospect's needs is important because it is only when you can gather relevant information and identify specific needs, that you can tailor a relevant and specific solution. If you haven't uncovered their needs, then what exactly are you providing a solution to?

The key to gathering the right information is to excel at effective questioning and active listening skills.

Effective questioning

The key to effective questioning is to have a process and prepare relevant questions for your prospect.

An effective questioning process

A mistake people often make when asking questions is to ask secondary questions before fully exploring the answers to the first. The key to effective questioning is to fully explore your prospect's response by listening to their answer then drilling down with further questions to gain a deeper understanding.

Drilling down

Think of drilling down as a process similar to a conversation about where you live. First you can name the continent you live on, then the country, then the state, the city, the suburb and the street – right down to your house number. With each piece of information you are getting more specific. If you follow this process in conversations with your prospect, you end up with a wealth of detailed and relevant information.

In a competitive context, if your competitor is gathering information about the prospect's challenges and needs at a general level (that is, from our example, at the continental level), while you are drilling down further (from our example, to the house-number level), you will have the advantage of greater information and the opportunity to provide a more precise and specific solution for your prospect.

The What, Which, Why technique

The concept of drilling down is based upon a specific questioning process: the What, Which, Why technique. The technique is used to establish *what* the key needs facing the prospect are, *which* of those needs are the most pressing and *why.* To make the most effective use of this technique, you need to have relevant question content.

Relevant content for questions

To have a meaningful conversation with your prospect, you need to have knowledge of relevant topics to discuss. The more information you have on your prospect and their business, the richer the conversation will be. Therefore, before you go to a meeting, thoroughly prepare questions from your research.

Start by asking your prospect a **What** question, such as:

- **What** outcomes are you looking to achieve with the brand launch?

Different industries will have sector-specific hot-button questions.

- **What** would need to happen for you to say that the brand launch was a success?

- **What** are some of the key challenges in launching your new brand?

Let's say your prospect answers your first question with:

> We want key influencers in the industry talking about the brand in a positive way and to generate sales.

At this moment, you may think you have the information you need to walk away and start writing a proposal to address your prospect's needs. However, further clarification and a deeper level of understanding can be obtained. You might then ask:

> You mentioned key influencers in the industry talking about the brand in a positive way. What exactly do you want them to be saying?

Let's say your prospect answers with:

> We want people saying that the brand is dynamic and delivers real benefits for the end user.

Both of these points must be explored further:

> You mentioned benefits for the end user; which benefits in particular? When you say dynamic, what does dynamic mean to you?

After you have fully explored their answers to each point, and you are satisfied that you have a complete understanding of each point, move on to exploring the next major point:

> *You also mentioned generating sales.*
> *Can I ask how many sales and over what timeframe?*

The key is to use their exact words, not your interpretation of them, to drill down further and deepen your level of understanding of your prospect's needs.

Useful probing questions

The following questions are useful probing questions in any conversation:

- *Can you tell me more?*

- *What is it about the situation that makes you say that?*

- *Can you give me an example?*

- *To what extent is it a problem?*

Now that you have explored your prospect's initial responses, you want to ensure that in the process you have uncovered all of your prospect's issues. This is important, as it is not uncommon for the key issue – the real problem – to be divulged at the end of the conversation, and sometimes not until you have suggested that something may be an issue. So you might want to ask:

You mentioned key influencers talking about the brand in a positive way in terms of it being dynamic and delivering real benefits for the end user; and secondly, generating $1million in sales over the next 12 months. Is there anything else you'd like to achieve besides those outcomes?

If they offer up another outcome, take the time to fully explore it. If they don't mention an issue you feel may be relevant, offer the issue for consideration:

You haven't mentioned your staff. Is using the launch to motivate staff a potential outcome?

Which and Why

Once the What questions have been uncovered and fully explored for deeper issues, you want to establish Which of the answers to the What questions are most important to the prospect and Why. You want to walk away with a clear idea of your prospect's most pressing challenges in order for you to tailor your presentation to address the issues in order of priority. Therefore, if your prospect doesn't offer the information, ask them:

• **Which** of these challenges do you see as the most important?

• **Why** is that?

Active listening

Throughout the drilling-down process, use active listening techniques to summarise and reaffirm what the prospect has just said. When listening:

- Stay focused and listen with the intent to really understand the issues

- Don't interrupt or complete the prospect's answers

- Don't think about your next question while the prospect is answering your current question

- Maintain eye contact, and use open and encouraging body language

- Take notes writing down key words only, so as not to break eye contact and rapport. (There is no point having a great conversation if you can't remember all the key points.)

Summarise what your prospect has said and repeat the information to them. Doing this ensures that you have understood what they are saying, and reaffirms for them your interest in their issues:

> *So if I understand correctly, what you are saying is that the key outcomes for the launch are...*

> *So if I understand you correctly, for the launch to be a success, the following needs to happen...*

Further questions that generate insight into the thought process and needs of your prospect include:

1. Asking questions about something that has happened

> *I noticed you recently advertised in magazine X. What was it about that magazine that particularly appealed to you?*

This question moves the conversation from the conceptual to the real. Their answer informs you of the factors that they take into consideration in their purchase decision – their buying process and what is important. If you can understand someone's buying process, it gives you clues how to sell to them. And if you know that you can deliver what is important to them, you know you are on the right track for a sale.

2. Asking comparative questions

You advertise in a range of magazines. Which ones would you say have been the most successful for your organisation?

This question again focuses on something that has happened and asks for a point of comparison to draw out further insight into what success looks like for your prospect. The answer to this question will again give you clues as to what's important for your prospect and the areas for you to address.

3. Asking decision-making questions

You need to find out the answers to:

- How decisions are made concerning budget or budget allocation

- What information your prospect bases his or her decision on

- What the budget is

You have nothing to lose by asking this last question. If you ask you may find out how much your prospect has to spend.

If you don't ask, you will never know. Once you do know, it is so much easier to provide a solution that meets their budgetary expectations.

Two classic mistakes when asking questions

The first classic mistake of poor questioners is introducing new words or content into the conversation when they are summarising and confirming what the prospect has said – language the prospect has not previously used. This gives the impression that you have not been listening properly.

The second classic mistake is leading the prospect. This is when the questioner provides two alternative scenarios to choose from, neither of which the prospect mentioned, then asks the prospect to choose which of the two is the key issue for their organisation. The prospect makes their choice of one of the two alternatives provided and the business developer incorrectly thinks that they now understand the challenges facing the prospect. It's like asking someone whether they prefer red or yellow, when their favourite colour is blue.

There is no need to make either of these mistakes. Simply ask the right questions, listen and reflect the prospect's language and words back to them. You want to maintain rapport with your prospect, not lose it.

KEY POINTS

- Questioning your prospect during your first meeting is a crucial stage, as it allows you to uncover your prospect's real needs

- Successful business developers – and interesting people – ask questions, so ask them!

EXERCISE

- Practise effective questioning and active listening on friends and colleagues in different situations

Notes

10

EXPLORING SOLUTIONS

Having uncovered your prospect's needs, move on to explore the solutions you can provide, to those needs, in order of importance.

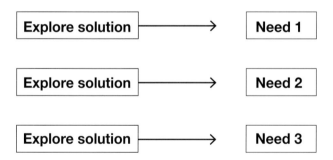

If this process is undertaken successfully in the meeting it will ensure that your proposal and presentation meet your prospect's needs.

Use a question to move into the exploration stage such as:

You said that the two key outcomes for the launch are, firstly, key influencers talking about the brand in a positive way in terms of it being dynamic and delivering real benefits for the end user; and secondly, generating $1 million in sales over the next 12 months. You also confirmed that the launch is an opportunity to motivate staff. If we could show you ways to achieve these outcomes and maximise the impact of the launch, is that something you would be interested in looking at?

Then you can move on to explore solutions to your prospect's needs in order of importance:

If we start with key influencers talking about the brand in a positive way in terms of it being dynamic and delivering real benefits for the end user, one idea we have is the following…

Outline your idea and then ask:

How does that sound?

Drill down and explore their response to establish what they like and dislike. Discuss together what would work best for them. Then move on to the next point.

In terms of the second outcome, generating sales…

Outline what you have done for another client and the results they achieved then ask:

If we could implement a similar program for you, would that be something you would like to explore in more detail?

Then you can enter into a discussion together about how your program – your solution – could work for them. Always gauge your prospect's reactions to your solutions, as this will confirm the elements that are right for your proposal and allow you to explore alternative solutions where necessary. This approach will allow you to shape your proposal into a 100% correct fit for them.

Seek permission to come back

After you have explored and agreed upon the solutions to your prospect's needs, seek their permission to come back and present the solution as a proposal, in person. Presenting in person allows you to observe their non-verbal reaction to what you have proposed, to further clarify points and to handle and overcome any objections.

KEY POINT

- Exploring and agreeing upon solutions during the first meeting with your prospect ensures that your proposal hits the mark

EXERCISE

- Practise the process of exploring solutions to your prospect's needs in your next business meeting

Notes

11 | PRESENTING COMPELLING SOLUTIONS

Having uncovered your prospect's needs and explored solutions in your first meeting, you are now in a position to present your fully considered proposal.

In some industries, a proposal might be presented verbally immediately after the business developer has uncovered his or her prospect's needs. However, the most common practice is for the solution to be delivered in another meeting in the form of a proposal and presentation. Your proposal provides the opportunity to both demonstrate your credentials to solve your prospect's issues and to reinforce your prospect's confidence that you are right for the job – some situations will call for a number of meetings until you are in a position to present a proposal.

Be aware that a problem with many proposals is demonstrating credentials rather than demonstrating an ability to solve the prospect's problems and address their needs. One of my clients told me how a number of advertising agencies were given an hour each to pitch for his company's business. My client was disappointed with the experience, telling me, 'Their pitches were all about their agency.' He said the agencies displayed examples of their work, discussed their clients and their philosophy, and talked about their strategic and creative capabilities.

The one thing the agencies failed to do was relate their experience and expertise to my client's needs.

'We' or 'You' presentation

The agencies' presentations were 'We' focused – *We do this, We do that* – rather than 'You' focused – *What this means for You.* This is not unusual. Most presentations I sit through are no different.

> *Your presentation should be about how you can address your prospect's needs, not about you*

How to develop a compelling, client-focused solution

The trick to developing compelling, client-focused solutions is not to work on the visual components of your presentation until you have a sound, logical argument in place of how you can help your prospect achieve their objectives. Construct your argument first and your visual aids second. The key to developing an effective argument is to use a planning chart.

Planning chart

To begin with, write each of your prospect's objectives in the left-hand column of the chart in order of priority. These will be the objectives you uncovered in the questioning stage.

Next, outline the features you can provide that can help your prospect achieve each objective and also note down the benefits that the features bring. Turn your features into benefits by using the phrase, *'Which means that…'*

In the final column, provide proof for your solution. Proof could include the use of testimonials, case studies, facts and figures and visual aids – a mixture of emotion and logic.

Here is an example of a potential objective being addressed in a planning chart:

Objectives	Features	Benefits	Proof
Our prospect needs to enhance relationships with their key clients and prospects.	We can provide them with an exclusive event for 100 of their top clients and prospects, with drinks and canapés and a tailored talk from the keynote speaker.	The client has the opportunity to build relationships in an exclusive environment, differentiating themselves from their competitors at the event and enhancing their position as industry leaders.	*Image of previous year's event. *Testimonial from a company who used a similar event to build relationships and drive business.

Work though the chart objective by objective, building up your logical argument. Once you have your logical argument planned, you can move on to develop your written proposal with confidence.

Put yourself in your prospect's position. How would you feel about a proposal that addresses your needs one by one compared to one that doesn't?

A variation on the theme

A variation on this approach in an actual presentation is to take each objective in turn and say the following:

Taking your first objective:

- *This is what we did for a client who had a similar challenge*

- *This was our approach and rationale at the time*

- *This was the result*

- *This is how that experience informs our approach to solving your problem*

- *This is our suggested approach and solution*

- *What are your thoughts regarding what we have proposed?*

From there, you can move on to their second objective, third objective and so on. The key is to address the prospect's needs in turn, providing them with solutions and showing them proof that you are the person to help them achieve their targets and objectives.

More on Proof

- Proof builds the prospect's **trust** in you, which is important as people buy trust first and products and services second

- Proof gives the prospect the required **confidence** to make the decision to move ahead with you

- Proof **differentiates** you from other organisations that make unsubstantiated claims about themselves. Take a look at any industry and pay attention to how many organisations describe themselves as 'industry leaders'

You can choose from four different types of proof to support your proposal.

1. Testimonials

A testimonial from a credible person or organisation can go a long way to building trust in the eyes of someone who has little or no experience of you. Ask for testimonials that describe not only the experience of working with you, but, more importantly, the problems that you addressed, the solutions you proposed and the results that were achieved as a result of working with you. Quantify the results where possible.

Here is an example of a helpful testimonial:

We had a real problem with motivation in the team. Jane worked with us over a number of months to understand the causes then developed and implemented a tailored program that addressed the core issues. As a direct result of Jane's work, the team is now significantly more focused and engaged, and sales are up 25% year on year. We are now working with Jane on rolling the program out across the organisation. Jane is incredibly professional and I highly recommend her services.

Use testimonials from an identifiable person and company ideally in the same industry as your prospect. A testimonial from J.P. from Texas or N.R. from London does not inspire the required level of trust and confidence. A helpful testimonial that clearly identifies your industry involvement may look like this:

The location was fantastic. Our clients said that it was the best venue that they had been to and the staff made everything so easy for us. We will be back next year.
– John Smith, Marketing Manager, ABCD Appliances

Such a testimonial is much more likely to attract your ideal client than saying:

We have 20 years experience in the industry.

The key with testimonials is to ask for them, not to wait for them to come to you. You could be waiting a long time. Make sure that the person you ask to provide a testimonial is someone that you are 100% comfortable about being approached by one of your prospects should they wish to delve further.

2. Case studies

Use case studies that go into detail about the challenges and needs a particular client had, and outline the solution you provided and the results that were achieved.

3. Facts and figures

Use relevant facts and figures to support your case. For example, ratings and demographics.

4. Visuals

Use images and videos where possible that provide a deeper understanding of the opportunity and show what your proposed solution will look like once it's implemented. Keep the videos short – no longer than five minutes.

Proposal and presentation structure

The key to a successful proposal whether it be in writing or delivered as a presentation is that it should mirror your verbal argument exactly. In doing so, your proposal must have a clear opening, body and closing argument.

Opening

The opening typically contains three key elements:

1. A cover page

The cover page contains a compelling sentence or statement that encapsulates the key outcome that your proposal will deliver. It entices the prospect to read on because the opportunity is directly related to helping them achieve their destined outcome *e.g. Successfully launching your new brand.*

2. What's in it for them (WIIFT)?

Provide your prospect with a summary of the key outcomes you are going to help them achieve. For example, you could summarise the key outcomes as:

- *Engaging key influencers in the industry*

- *Positioning your brand as dynamic and delivering real benefits for the end user*

- *Generating $1 million in sales over the next 12 months*

- *Motivating your staff*

3. Agenda

The agenda will summarise what you are going to cover in the proposal or presentation.

Body

The main body of your proposal or presentation is where you will inform and persuade your prospect. Break down the information into digestible chunks and demonstrate a logical argument showing how you will meet their objectives. Emphasise the points you know they will be interested in from your research and previous discussions. The body of your proposal or presentation should contain the following elements:

1. Organisation and product, service or event

Give a brief overview of your organisation providing pertinent information in key point format. The amount of information you provide will depend on your prospect's current knowledge of your organisation and the information you provide will vary depending on your industry. A good starting point is to address the questions as follows: *who, what, why, how, where, when* and *how long.*

- Who we are – your name and legal entity

- What we do – the nature of your work

- Why we do it – your mission and purpose and the need you address

- How we do it – your approach, solutions and values

- Where we do it – geographical locations and online locations

- When we do it – times and dates

- How long we have been doing it – when you commenced business

Similar questions should then be addressed for the specific product, service or event that you want your prospect to engage with.

2. Objectives/outcomes

Using the information in your planning chart on page 81, address each of your prospect's objectives in turn in your proposal – present the information in the following form, addressing one objective per page.

Objective →	**Enhance relationships with key clients and prospects.**	**Proof** ↓
Benefits →	The opportunity to build relationships in an exclusive environment, differentiate yourselves from your competitors and enhance your position as an industry leader.	*Insert image of previous year's event *Testimonial from a company who used a similar event to build relationships and drive business
Features →	• An exclusive event for 100 of your top clients and prospects • Drinks and canapés • A tailored talk from the keynote speaker	

3. Timings

Include an activity timeline outlining the next steps, what is required to take the next steps and who will be actioning each point.

4. Making it happen

Outline the team that is going to make your prospect's objectives happen in your organisation. Provide the prospect with your team members' names, roles, experience and photos if possible.

5. Credentials

Provide further evidence in terms of the outcomes you will generate, the other clients you have on board as well as similar projects you have completed.

6. Measurement

Outline how you intend to measure achievement against your objectives, and suggest various means by which your prospect can measure their success for themselves.

7. Investment

Outline the overall investment required in terms of dollars and the duration of the agreement.

Closing argument

1. Summary

Revisit what's in it for them. This is where you reiterate the outcomes they are going to receive, first highlighted in sections 1 and 2 of the presentation or proposal opening.

2. Appendix

This typically contains detailed information referenced in the proposal or presentation, for example, product specifications, media schedules, and legal agreements.

Key messages, the big picture and lifetime value

Three important elements often missing from a proposal or presentation are:

• Delivering the key messages

• Selling the big picture before the detail

• Selling the lifetime value, not the price

1. Key messages

When I critique proposals, too often I am left wondering as to what the real opportunity – the big idea or proposition – is for the prospect. If I can't see it then neither will your prospect. Invariably, the key messages are woven into the narrative of the proposal to such an extent that they can't be seen. The trick is to use headings, subheadings and visual aids throughout your proposal to bring the key messages to the fore.

2. Sell the big picture before the detail

Ensure that your prospect has bought into the overall benefit of what you are proposing before you sell them your specific opportunity.

In the case of the exhibition company, if they don't first sell their prospect on the broader benefits of exhibiting, they then leave themselves open to the objection from the prospect that they just don't see the value in exhibiting at all, let alone your opportunity.

Once the prospect has agreed on the overall benefits of involvement, you can then confidently discuss which specific opportunity is best suited to their needs. Taking this approach will significantly reduce the number of objections you receive and will increase your success rate.

3. Selling lifetime value, not the price

In presenting your solution to your prospect, you'll need to demonstrate the value in what you are proposing. One way to do that is to communicate the potential lifetime value that your proposal can deliver to your prospect.

Lifetime value is the value of one client multiplied by the length of time that the client stays with you.

To identify the potential lifetime value, ask your prospect the following:

- *What is the typical dollar value of one of their clients?*

- *How long do their clients stay with them on average?*

- *What are their prospect-to-client conversion rates?*

Value of client
x
number of years
= lifetime value

Let's say that the answers to these questions are $10,000, five years and that for every fifty prospects they meet at an event they gain five meetings and convert one new client.

The key is to get your prospect to see that if they were to secure just one client from your opportunity, the lifetime value of that client to their organisation would be $50,000 ($10,000 x 5 years). Given the size of the audience at the event, based on their conversion rate ratios (see Chapter 3) if they were to meet 250 qualified prospects they could potentially obtain twenty-five meetings and convert five new clients. This would mean a $250,000 return. If your original investment was $20,000 this would be a good Return On Investment (ROI) in anyone's books.

A similar technique is to demonstrate the value of what you are proposing in terms of what your prospect will save. Again, using the exhibition example, the approach would be to convey the proposition of exhibiting:

The opportunity here is to engage the key decision-makers in your industry in one location over three days in an environment where they are looking for new products and ideas, and to do business.

Then, using your questioning skills, ask the prospect:

- *How long would it take you to visit all the delegates individually, away from the conference?*

- *How much would that activity cost? Consider the flights, accommodation and ground transfers.*

- *Could you guarantee your prospect's availability for a meeting?*

The key in asking all these questions is to let your prospect answer the questions. As they do, they will understand the real value of your proposal and they will be selling your solution to themselves.

(This technique can also be used to overcome the ROI objection. For more information about ROI, see Chapter 12.)

KEY POINTS

The key to providing a compelling solution is to:

- Address each of your prospect's challenges and needs in turn

- Outline your solution for each

- Provide the relevant evidence to back up each solution.

In your proposal or presentation be sure to:

- Communicate key messages

- Sell the big picture and broader benefits before the detail

- Sell the lifetime value, not the price

EXERCISES

In developing your next solution, ask yourself:

- Have you clearly identified your prospect's objectives?

- Have you built a logical argument to meet their objectives?

- Have you provided the relevant proof to back up each solution?

- Can you approach previous clients and ask them to provide a testimonial?

There is more information about how to present proposals effectively on my website:

www.richardwoodward.com.au

Notes

12 | CLOSING THE SALE

Now that you have presented your solution to your prospect, you need to close the sale with them and have your prospect say 'yes' to what you have proposed.

Many people mistake closing the sale as the endpoint of the sales process, where a phrase or technique is pulled out of the bag to secure the prospect. However, if you have not built rapport, uncovered a prospect's real needs and presented a compelling solution, no magic words or techniques will close the sale for you – instead, you may receive a mass of objections.

For the prospect, observing a salesperson trying to close a deal with them when these landmarks have not been achieved can be both annoying and amusing.

Build commitment along the way

While there has to be an inducement to action, closing is about gaining commitment at every stage of the business development process. You need to gain your prospect's commitment to meet; then gain their commitment to a solution; then gain their commitment to proceed to the next stage.

The key to gaining your prospect's commitment is to focus on successfully completing each stage of the process in turn, such as building rapport, uncovering needs and exploring possible solutions rather than thinking that you can rush to the endpoint and leave with a sale. By taking this approach, you will take pressure off yourself during the interaction, and the inducement to action – the close – becomes a natural and expected part of the process.

Buying signals

The good news is that throughout the interaction, your prospect will give off either positive or negative buying signals. When you learn to recognise these signals, you can establish how near or far your prospect is from committing to you, and this knowledge can help you work out what to say or do next.

Positive signals

Positive buying signals may be given verbally and non-verbally. Positive verbal buying signals include your prospect asking for more specific, detailed information, as well as talking about how they would implement the solution you are proposing, such as discussing who they would get to do the keynote speech and which clients they would invite. Pay attention to how the prospect speaks: other verbal positive buying signals include increased vocal pace and tone.

Non-verbal positive buying signals include nodding in agreement with your suggestions and matching your body language. For example, if you are leaning forward as you express a point, your prospect may also lean forward.

Negative signals

Negative buying signals may also be given verbally and non-verbally. Asking you how long the meeting will take and whether you have much further to go may suggest frustration or an increasing lack of interest in your pitch.

Negative non-verbal buying signals include losing and avoiding eye contact as well as breaking rapport in body language.

Calibration

Don't mistake an enthusiastic person as being a prospect exhibiting positive buying signals. Your prospect may be enthusiastic in all types of situations. Ideally, try to read their behaviour in your initial discussion and calibrate their ongoing behaviour and temperament against it as the proposal proceeds.

How to respond

Your job as a business developer is to read the buying signals and respond accordingly. If I am observing positive buying signals from my prospect, I'll use a very open question such as, *What are your thoughts at this stage?*, to which my prospect may respond with, *I like it.* In response, I may drill deeper with, *Can I ask, what is it exactly that you like?* If your prospect then tells you that your solution matches their objectives, you know you are on the right track and can proceed with confidence towards closing the sale.

Closing the sale: inducing action

Here are five strong techniques you can employ for inducing action and closing the sale with your prospect.

1. Ask them!

Ask your prospect if they would like to go ahead with your proposal. If they want to go ahead, and if you have followed the rest of the process correctly, why wouldn't they want to proceed? If they say yes, that's good news. And if they don't say yes, then you will need to work towards overcoming their objections. Remember, at this point you are still in the game. You just need to do some more work.

2. Give them a choice

Provide your prospect with a choice of options. Make sure your offers are realistic and can be followed through.

We can give you a position next to the entrance or near the stage. Both areas will have high traffic flow. Which one would you prefer?

3. The next steps

To give you maximum exposure in the event program, we are going to need your logo by next Friday. Is that achievable?

This is a great technique for anyone with a solution that is time-critical, such as an event or program to be held on specific dates. The key is to position the next steps for your prospect's benefit, not yours. Asking your prospect what they see as the next steps can often lead to them communicating his or her commitment to proceed.

4. Scarcity/competition

This technique plays upon your prospect's fear of their competition and by establishing deadlines reinforces the need for activity and closing the sale.

As you would appreciate, we'll be talking to a number of other companies about this opportunity. However, if you are interested, we can hold the position for you until the end of the week, but we would need a decision by then as we are expecting significant industry interest.

5. Provide an opportunity to involve them in the implementation

Providing an opportunity for your prospect to be involved in the implementation of your solution is the least-direct technique, but can be quite useful for moving your prospect towards closing the sale.

We are talking to our agency on Thursday. Why don't you come along and we can explore some ideas for maximising your involvement?

Following your suggestion, your prospect may respond positively with, *Yes, that sounds like a good idea,* which indicates that you are getting nearer to commitment. Or, if you receive a look that says, *What would we do that for? We are not interested,* then you will want to address their negative signals.

Whichever technique you use to induce action and close the sale, once your prospect has agreed to move ahead, you may like to say something like, *Great – I will get the contract across to you tomorrow.*

Deliver with confidence

The key is to deliver your words with confidence, no matter which technique you use. Your confidence will give your prospect confidence to proceed. Now is not the time to hesitate!

Encountering negative signals

If you are encountering negative buying signals, gently ask your prospect questions to determine the extent of the problem. Use words and phrases that feel natural to you. I use:

I am getting a sense that we are not addressing your issues. Would I be right?, or, *Am I right in thinking that what we propose is not hitting the spot for you?*

If your observations are correct and your prospect indicates that your proposal is not meeting their objectives, you can perhaps say:

Which of the things that are important to you do you feel we are not addressing?

Once you hear your prospect's response, you now have the opportunity to address their objections in turn.

Overcoming objections

What separates successful from less successful business developers is how they respond to client objections. Successful business developers know that an objection is a cue to ask more questions, not a cue to end the conversation. If you end the conversation upon hearing an objection, you miss out on the opportunity to turn your prospect's objection into a sale.

The key to successfully overcoming any objection is to:

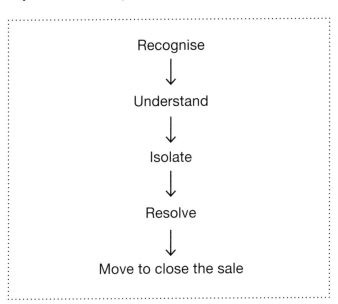

Recognise
↓
Understand
↓
Isolate
↓
Resolve
↓
Move to close the sale

Let's look at three classic objections and explore how we would respond to them:

1. We don't have any budget.
2. It doesn't provide enough ROI.
3. I'm too busy – can you just send me a proposal?

How to respond to '*We don't have any budget.*'

We don't have any budget is one of the classic objections that I am sure we have all experienced at some point in time. A mistake many people make is to conclude the lack of budget is the only thing stopping the prospect from saying yes to your proposal. This is often not the case. Here are the five steps to overcoming the budget objection.

1. Recognise the objection

First of all, recognise that your prospect has an objection. This demonstrates you are listening to them and, in turn, maintains rapport. Say something like:

Obviously budget is an important consideration.

2. Understand the objection

Demonstrate your concern by seeking to understand your prospect's objection. Establish which budget and which financial year they are referring to:

When you say you have no budget, can I ask which budget are you referring to? And which financial year budget are you referring to?

Your prospect's answers will give you insight into how to resolve their objection.

3. Isolate the objection

The key to resolving your prospect's budget objection is to ensure that it is a real objection and the only thing stopping them from moving forward with you. If it's not, solving the budget objection won't get you a sale. You may want to ask:

Is there anything else besides budget that is stopping you moving ahead?

If the answer is no, you can move on to say:

So if we can address your concerns about budget, is there any other reason why you can't proceed? Will you be in a position to move ahead?

A question I find to be really effective in this situation is to ask the prospect:

If you had the budget, would you go ahead?

The answer to this question offers greater insight as to whether budget is the real objection for the prospect. If budget is the real objection, you can still work towards resolving it. If it's not, then it allows you to uncover and address what is really stopping your prospect from committing.

4. Resolve the objection

By establishing which financial year your prospect is referring to with their budget concern, you can work to resolve the objection by exploring different payment options. You may like to suggest they spread the payments out over a longer period, or perhaps that they might consider accessing alternative budgets to support the proposal. For example, if your prospect says that they are referring to their sponsorship budget when they say they have no budget, this gives you the chance to overcome their objection by pointing out that the opportunity provides a marketing platform comprising advertising, brand and business development benefits. If they see value in the opportunity and budget is the only thing stopping them from moving ahead, perhaps they could consider accessing their advertising, brand or business development budget to implement the opportunity.

5. Move to close the sale

At this point, use one of the inducement techniques outlined earlier in the chapter to close the sale.

How to respond to 'It doesn't provide enough ROI'

Another common objection is:

It doesn't provide enough ROI.

When people hear this objection, some incorrectly launch straight into a repeat of the key features and benefits that their proposal offers the prospect, thinking that by repeating what they have said, they will win over the prospect. Remember, the prospect heard you the first time. Instead, apply the following five-step process:

1. Recognise the objection

Recognise that your prospect has an objection. Show that you are listening to them and maintain rapport. Say something like:

Of course, it is vitally important that you achieve a return from any investment.

2. Understand the objection

Demonstrate your concern by seeking to understand your prospect's objection. In this instance, the challenge is that ROI means different things to different people. For some, good ROI might mean greater prospects, sales and revenue. For others, good ROI might mean more press coverage, enhanced brand awareness and reputation, or greater access to unique experiences and hospitality opportunities.

Not only does ROI mean different things to different people, but within each answer is a whole range of more specific questions. For example, if your prospect sees ROI in terms of increased sales, the questions are then:

ROI is whatever ROI means for that prospect.

- *Sales of which products?*

- *In which market?*

- *Over what timeframe?*

So you might want to ask your prospect:

When you say ROI, what does ROI mean to you in your business?

Then drill down on their answers to gather more information.

3. Isolate the objection

If you establish that your prospect's concern is a fear over lack of ROI – say, that there will not be enough sales of a specific product over a specific timeframe – you need to ensure that this objection is the only concern stopping your prospect from moving ahead. You might want to ask them:

Besides your concern that there will not be enough sales over the timeframe, is there anything else that is stopping you moving ahead?

If the answer is no, move on to resolving the objection.

4. Resolve the objection

One way to resolve your prospect's objection over concerns about ROI would be to demonstrate how others have achieved outstanding sales and, in particular, what they did to achieve those results. You could suggest to your prospect that you can work with them on putting together a plan on how to effectively maximise their ROI.

Another solution might be to get your prospect to see the lifetime value potential of new clients that can be achieved from your proposal. (For further information on establishing lifetime value potential, see Chapter 11.)

5. Move to close the sale

At this point, use one of the inducement techniques outlined earlier in the chapter to close the sale.

How to respond to '*I'm too busy – can you just send me a proposal?*'

If a prospect responds to your phone call by cutting to: '*Can you just send me a proposal?*', this is not technically an objection, as you have not yet had the chance to present your prospect with your solution. If you followed the rest of the process correctly, you should not be placed in this position by your prospect. If you ever get this from a prospect early on in the sales process, it may be worth exploring how to react.

Participants in my workshops tell me that the incidence of winning business after responding to such a request from a prospect is low. Worse still, other work is put on hold while precious time is taken to carefully prepare and dispatch the proposal.

The key is to take control of the situation by requesting a face-to-face meeting or, at best, continuing the dialogue over the phone while the person is available to talk. So you might respond by saying:

I could send you a proposal. However, you probably get inundated with proposals that don't meet your needs. I imagine that the last thing you want is another proposal like that. Would that be right? So what I would like to do is to ask you a few questions about your objectives. Then I can put together some suggestions that will really help you. Perhaps we can arrange for a brief meeting later this week?

While at first you might think that it is strange to turn down an invitation to send a proposal, there are benefits to this approach:

- You increase your credibility with the prospect by taking the time to find out what it is they are trying to achieve

- You give yourself greater opportunity to fashion something that relates to what they are really looking for

- You don't waste your time or energy writing and sending proposals that have little chance of being taken up

- You don't waste the mental space on a prospect that might not be right for you

> Above all, remember: *Some people will get you. Some won't. Find those that do and don't worry about those that don't.* If your prospect denies you a meeting and insists on a written proposal, maybe this is not your ideal client and you need to move on to find the person who is.

How would you feel?

One of my favourite techniques that seems to really hit the spot for clients if delivered at the appropriate time and in the right manner is what I call the 'How would you feel' technique.

This technique is used when you are presenting an attractive opportunity to a prospect who has a key competitor and where the prospect requires a little more persuasion to get them across the line.

Get your prospect to imagine their competitor implementing the opportunity. Let's say you are pitching an opportunity to your prospect to sponsor an event where many customers and potential customers will be present. Consider asking your prospect questions such as:

How would you feel walking into the event and seeing your competitor's signage and their marketing director on stage addressing your customers and potential customers? What would the audience be thinking and feeling about your competitor at that moment?

Or if you are pitching a prospect the opportunity to advertise in a program or magazine, consider asking them questions such as:

How would you feel picking up the program and seeing your competitor's advert engaging your clients and prospects? What would your clients and prospects be thinking and feeling about your competitors at that moment?

You know that the situations you are describing are not desirable for your prospect – but don't leave it there.

Probe to generate a deeper understanding

Ask probing questions to understand specifically why it would be an unattractive situation for your prospect. Draw out from your prospect exactly what advantages their competitor would be gaining.

Help the prospect see the opportunity from a different perspective

By getting your prospect to look at the opportunity from a different perspective – that is, how the opportunity would benefit their key competitor – it will help your prospect to see the benefits of their own involvement and sell the opportunity, in essence doing your job for you.

It's all in the delivery

To achieve the desired effect, the 'How would you feel' question should be delivered in a manner indicating a genuine desire to help the prospect see the opportunity from a different perspective. If this can be achieved, the technique can be a defining moment in a presentation.

KEY POINTS

- Building commitment at every stage of the sales process is the key to achieving an effective sale. If you do this, then the close will be a natural and expected part of the process

- Objections are a cue to ask more questions, not a cue to end the conversation

EXERCISES

- Practise observing positive and negative verbal and non-verbal signals in meetings. Calibrate your prospect's behaviour against previous conversations

- Try different closing techniques to find the ones that work best for you in your business

- Practise five-step responses for overcoming objections you receive from your prospects

Notes

Notes

13 | SERVICING & RETAINING CLIENTS

Once you have closed the sale, your prospect now converts into your client. In business development practice, too much emphasis is often placed on the final stage of securing a prospect as a client, with too little emphasis on servicing and retaining them into the future. Unfortunately, many business developers typically secure a client, implement what was agreed in the proposal then, towards the end of the process, realise they have to re-sell their opportunities all over again. The key to client retention is effective servicing throughout the process.

Effective servicing takes place at two levels

People like to do business with organisations that can solve their problems as well as with people they like. Effective service takes place at these two levels.

1. Effective servicing at an organisation level

Deliver what you promised

As a bare minimum, you must deliver what you promised, ideally exceeding your new client's expectations and, of course, providing a positive experience.

Help them achieve their business outcomes

Help your new client to integrate the features you have sold them into their ongoing business activities to drive home real benefits and outcomes.

> *The best marketing you can ever do is to do a great job for an existing client*

For example, if your client has used hospitality entitlements to entertain potential prospects, discuss with your client how they are going to follow up on those new relationships and move the prospects through their sales pipeline. Provide advice on how best to do so, using examples of what your other clients have done and discussing measures of success.

Understand and show interest in their business

Effective servicing is about continually looking at your new client's business to uncover additional needs to which you can provide a solution. In essence, the sales mindset that you had up to the point of your client's conversion continues throughout the servicing phase.

Find out what issues are impacting on your client's industry and engage them in a conversation on how the issues will challenge their business. Your client should experience you continually trying to understand their needs, finding solutions to their problems and seeking to help their business.

Don't be afraid to challenge your client's thinking. Have them consider various options. Make their time spent with you a valuable and informative experience worth repeating.

Show initiative

Send articles to your new client relating to their industry or competitors for their information or send a timeline of matters affecting their sector over the next few years. Such gestures provide topics to focus on during your next conversation.

Deliver a complete and positive end-to-end experience

Ensure that every interaction or touch-point you have with your new client from start to finish, whether large or small, meets and exceeds their expectations. Too often a business will lose custom because one aspect of the experience was so bad it coloured what was otherwise an okay experience.

First, map out the sequence of interactions that you have with your clients, noting down each stage of the experience they will have with you, particularly points where you have the potential to either delight or frustrate. Be as specific as possible – ensure every stage is included.

Second, consider how you can improve their experience at each stage. Importantly, ask your clients about their current experience of you and the ways they think it can be improved. Very few organisations do this effectively. Hotels may give out feedback forms, but how often as a customer do you fill those in? If you really want feedback from a client, pick up the phone and ask them. Better still, get a face-to-face meeting with them and ask your question with a genuine desire to find out the answer and with a view to making improvements.

Third, take the necessary steps to improve the experience you deliver in the areas required.

In taking this plan of action, you will ensure – rather than hope – that you are delivering a positive experience that delights your clients. You might not want to hear some of the feedback. But isn't it better to find out the areas that are putting your relationship at risk and secure the opportunity to take action for the better, rather than carry on believing everything is fine?

Stay in touch

We only hear from them when they want to sell us something.

Avoid overhearing this comment. Construct a program to stay in touch with your clients and provide customers with something of value throughout the year such as monthly tips or invitations to seminars and hospitality events, or using various social media platforms to keep your client engaged.

Move from being a seller to your client's confidential advisor

Move from being simply a seller of products or services to being your new client's confidential advisor. You know you have achieved this when your client shares information with you about what is really going on in their business and seeks your input on how to deal with new challenges.

2. Effective servicing at a personal level

Make the experience of working with you at a personal level enjoyable by making your client feel special. Provide your client with unique experiences that have valuable meaning and relevance for them. Not everyone wants to attend a golf day! But they may have more interest in listening to a professional golfer share experiences on maximising performance which can be applied to business. Also, make your client look influential by providing them with information of value they can then pass on to their colleagues.

Tools for ensuring retention

Here are five key tools for ensuring success during the client servicing and retention phase.

1. Joint implementation plan

Together with your client, develop a joint implementation plan (JIP) that sets up a relationship for success. Outline who does what and when, and the agreed measureable outcomes to be achieved.

2. Regular reviews

Your JIP should provide a format for regular joint review to determine what's working, what's not and what either you or your client could do differently.

In review sessions, you can use an assumptive close to re-sign the client without having to necessarily re-pitch. The key is to explore suggestions for improvement in the following year or next agreement then say, *I will put these points into a new agreement and send it over to you in the morning for signing off.* Essentially, you are assuming that the client will be going ahead with you again without explicitly asking them. This tactic sidesteps having to re-pitch.

The importance of effective servicing – the lifetime value of retaining a client

Effective servicing and retention ensures you retain the important lifetime dollar value generated from a satisfied long-term client. Therefore your mindset and approach must be focused on servicing to the lifetime value potential of the client at all times, not the initial transaction amount.

Service your client to the lifetime value amount, not the initial transaction amount.

Imagine for a moment you owned a coffee shop and a new customer walked in. What level of service would you give them? If you view the customer as another person buying a $3 coffee and don't deliver great service, you could miss out on around $1,500 from that one regular customer over a two-year period. Multiply that figure over a number of customers and you have the difference between a thriving business and one going bust.

In business development, you must service your clients on each and every visit as if they will become a $1,500 coffee customer, not just another $3 customer. Every time you service for the sale price and not the lifetime value, you give your clients reason to go elsewhere. You will then have to spend more time, money and effort attracting new prospects – and the unprofitable cycle continues. The level of service you deliver will determine the lifetime value you derive.

3. Effective questioning

Use your drilling-down questioning skills and your active listening skills to determine your client's level of satisfaction with regard to the service you are delivering.

4. Leveraging workshops

Undertake workshops with your client to explore and identify what else both parties can do to drive additional value from the relationship.

5. Joint client workshops

Bring several of your clients together and facilitate a workshop to explore and identify opportunities for them to do business with each other.

KEY POINTS

- Long-term client retention requires a focused service plan extending beyond the initial implementation of your solution

- Service to the lifetime value potential of your client, not to the initial transaction amount

EXERCISE

- Develop a written and robust Service and Retention Plan that will ensure the delivery of lifetime value to your organisation

Notes

14

MAXIMISING PERFORMANCE

During the business development process, when prospects don't return your calls and/or decline your proposals, you can experience a blow to your confidence that may contribute to a negative, non-resourceful state of mind. This impact is amplified if you are operating in a long sales cycle where a fair amount of time elapses between wins. State management – managing your mindset to achieve the task in hand – will ensure that you are confident and resourceful at all times. It is vital to give yourself the best shot at success.

Here are seven techniques that will help you to attain and retain a positive and confident mindset throughout the business development process and help you maximise your performance.

1. Preparation and practise

Preparation and practise can improve your performance by 100%. If you're going to deliver a presentation and you don't prepare and practise, I guarantee you won't give your best performance or achieve the best outcome. If you do prepare and practise, I guarantee that it will enhance your confidence and you will deliver a more effective presentation every time.

I observe this each time I run a two-day presentation skills course. The people who take the time and put in the effort overnight to prepare and practise for their presentation experience a marked improvement in their performance the following day.

There are a number of elements in the business development process you can prepare for, the most obvious being phone calls, meetings and presentations.

Phone calls

Preparing for a phone call involves:

- Preparing the structure and content of your call

- Researching the company in order to have meaningful dialogue

- Considering likely objections you'll receive and how to overcome them. (For further information on preparing for a phone call, see Chapter 5.)

Meetings

Preparing for a meeting involves:

- Establishing your objectives and what you will take away from the meeting

- Outlining your process for the meeting such as building rapport, uncovering needs and exploring solutions

- Preparing questions that will generate discussion as well as preparing answers to questions you might be asked. (For further information on preparing for a sales meeting, see Chapter 7.)

Presentations

Preparing for a presentation involves:

- Ensuring you have a clear understanding of your audience and who will be at the meeting

- Checking the room set-up

- Preparing your presentation structure and visual aids

Practise simply means rehearsal: practise your presentation out loud, role-play the phone call and the meeting, practise your questioning techniques and methods of overcoming objections.

The more often you practise, the better your performance will be.

2. Reassociate with positive experiences

Before any meeting, phone call or presentation you have with your prospect, recall a similar interaction that went well and reassociate with that positive experience by seeing what you saw, hearing what you heard and feeling what you felt at the time. By doing this, you bring the positive experience from the past into the present.

3. Visualise the outcomes you want

Pre-program your subconscious mind to achieve the outcome you want. In the same way that a soccer player visualises the ball going into the back of the net, visualise yourself confidently walking into a meeting, shaking hands, making eye contact, building rapport, asking meaningful questions and exploring solutions with your future client.

4. Play music

Music is an instant mood changer. Before any interaction with a prospect, play music to get you into the state of mind that will deliver your best performance for the occasion. Music can be used either as a stimulant or to calm your nerves. It allows you to create internal focus, taking attention away from any external focus.

I have particular pieces of music that I play before a presentation. Every time I hear them, they trigger an association with the positive feelings of a successful presentation. For training sessions, I have different pieces that trigger an association with running a successful training session.

5. Get physical

Consider the physical aspects of performance. Looking after your fitness will improve both your mental clarity and physical wellbeing.

Exercise

After I exercise, my mind is clear, I feel good and I can perform at my best. I would rather commit to an hour of exercise then interact with clients for five hours in a positive state of mind than interact with clients for six hours, foregoing the hour of exercise, and not performing at my best.

Physical posture

Be aware of your physical posture at all times. Adopt a confident posture in meetings, presentations and on the phone. Consider making phone calls standing up rather than sitting down.

6. Reconnect with your purpose and vision

Reconnect with the purpose and vision that you had when you joined your organisation or set up your business. Remember why you chose to do what you do. Read inspiring quotations or passages by an author who has travelled a similar path to the one that you want to travel. Consider how your role models would behave in your situation.

7. Proof

Read testimonials you have received and look at your client list: both prove that you can achieve the outcomes you want to achieve. If you have attracted one client, there is no reason you can't attract another. If you have delivered great outcomes for one client, you can do the same for others. Keep a journal capturing the positive feedback you receive from clients, as it is another reference point of proof.

Tracking success

Tracking your success and learning from your experiences to improve your game are vital ingredients for maximising performance. Track the success of your business development activity by measuring the number of prospects, meetings and clients generated through action. Tracking your success allows you to evaluate the success of the time, effort and budget you've spent in engaging your ideal clients and effectively allocate resources for the following year.

Learn from positive and negative experiences to enhance your performance

Every activity you undertake in the business development process – presenting, pitching, making appointments, networking and meeting prospects – provides you with an opportunity to learn from the experience and enhance your performance.

A simple and powerful process to improve your performance

After each activity you undertake in the process, take a moment to ask yourself:

- What went well that I need to do again next time?

- What didn't go so well that I need to change next time?

- What am I going to do differently next time?

Give yourself the opportunity to improve

If you ask yourself these questions at the end of each experience, you create the opportunity to enhance your performance. Like the workshop participant who sent out fifty letters with no success so she sent out fifty more, if you don't ask yourself questions and evaluate your own performance, you risk repeating unsuccessful actions and the chances are your results will remain the same.

Learning from the things that go well

Let's say you observed that the research you undertook on a prospect prior to meeting allowed you to engage in a more meaningful conversation about their business. The experience reinforced the link between researching your prospects and productive meetings with prospects. So, what are you going to do? Ensure that you undertake research before every meeting.

Learning from the things that didn't go well

Let's say you left a meeting unsure about the real needs of your prospect. You replay the meeting in your mind and recall that you didn't confirm back to the prospect your understanding of their needs at the end of the meeting. The experience tells you the importance of active listening and of confirming back to ensure that you have clearly understood their needs. So, now what are you going to do? Commit to undertake confirming back at every meeting and to spend time practising this skill.

Regular reviews

The process of reviewing and learning from your own experience can be undertaken after each interaction and at various times, such as monthly, quarterly and annually. When I facilitate teams through the review process on their planning days, the learning gained and the impact on driving their business and organisation forward can be immense.

The advantages of this approach

The small improvements that you make activity by activity, day by day and month by month over the course of a year will lead to a significant increase in your performance. Your performance, like a snowball, will gather momentum. The larger it gets, the faster it goes.

KEY POINT

- Attaining and retaining a confident, positive mindset and learning from your experiences to drive performance are two crucial elements for success

EXERCISES

- Practise the techniques listed in this chapter to achieve a positive, confident state and maximise your performance

- Undertake regular reviews to debrief your own experiences and drive learning and improved performance

Notes

Well, there it is! Business Development that works. Now it's up to you. Now it's about action: your action. On the following pages I have provided a summary of each chapter and a page for you to outline what you are going to stop doing, start doing and continue doing moving forward.

Remember:

Some people will get you. Some won't. Find those that do and don't worry about those who don't.

So get to it, and good luck!

SUMMARY

Chapter 1 Identifying your ideal client

- Developing clarity on who you want to work with – your ideal client – is the starting point for success in business development

- Saying no to people and opportunities that do not represent your ideal client is essential to your success

Chapter 2 Developing your proposition

- Developing a clear and concise proposition – your elevator pitch – gives you the opportunity to attract your ideal clients

- Constantly develop and fine tune your ptich

Chapter 3 Finding prospects

- Your future clients and success are determined by the activities you undertake today

- Develop a realistic, written and robust business development activity plan that outlines exactly where you can find prospective clients. With consistent effort behind it, your plan will give you the momentum to achieve your targets

Chapter 4 Refining prospects

- Your future success is determined by the quality and quantity of your prospect list, and the research you undertake today

- The more information you can find on the business and personal hot buttons of your prospect, the more you can tailor an approach that is likely to result in positive outcomes

Chapter 5 Approaching prospects

- The key to successfully approaching a prospect is to tailor your content and delivery to the world of the prospect and to focus on the relevant outcomes you can deliver for them

Chapter 6 Attracting prospects

- Attraction activities are a powerful way of drawing the right prospects to you. Attraction activities provide the opportunity to *demonstrate* your expertise and for your ideal clients to *experience* you

Chapter 7 Preparing for a sales meeting

- Preparing for a meeting will greatly enhance your success in the meeting

Chapter 8 Building rapport

- Take the time to build rapport. It will help you to develop trust and understanding with your prospect

- Build rapport by 'joining the world' of your prospect

Chapter 9 Uncovering needs

- Questioning your prospect during your first meeting is a crucial stage, as it allows you to uncover your prospect's real needs

- Successful business developers – and interesting people – ask questions, so ask them!

Chapter 10 Exploring solutions

- Exploring and agreeing upon solutions during the first meeting with your prospect ensures that your proposal hits the mark

Chapter 11 Presenting compelling solutions

The key to providing a compelling solution is to:

- Address each of your prospect's challenges and needs in turn

- Outline your solution for each

- Provide the relevant evidence to back up each solution

In your proposal or presentation be sure to:

- Communicate key messages

- Sell the big picture and broader benefits before the detail

- Sell the lifetime value, not the price

Chapter 12 Closing the sale

- Building commitment at every stage of the sales process is the key to achieving an effective sale. If you do this, then the close will be a natural and expected part of the process

- Objections are a cue to ask more questions, not a cue to end the conversation

Chapter 13 Servicing and retaining clients

- Long-term client retention requires a focused service plan extending beyond the initial implementation of your solution

- Service to the lifetime value potential of your client, not to the initial transaction amount

Chapter 14 Maximising performance

- Attaining and retaining a confident, positive mindset and learning from your experiences to drive performance are two crucial elements for success

Actions

What am I going to:

- Stop doing

- Start doing

- Continue doing

Notes

CONTACT

To:

- Book Richard to speak at your conference and/or facilitate your strategy day

- Discuss training needs in your organisation

- Receive Richard's monthly business development tips

- Stay in touch with Richard through LinkedIn, Twitter and YouTube

visit www.richardwoodward.com.au